GIRL TO GIRL

Friends and You!

Anne Driscoll

Illustrated by
Raymond Turvey

SCHOLASTIC INC.

New York   Toronto   London   Auckland   Sydney
Mexico City   New Delhi   Hong Kong

To the special ones who have loved me,
listened to me, supported me, stuck by me,
cried with me, cared for me, been with me and
been there for me. To my friends.

ISBN 0-439-26767-6

12 11 10 9 8 7 6 5 4 3 2   1 2 3 4 5/0

Printed in the U.S.A.   40

First Scholastic printing, December 2000

Cover design by Mandy Sherliker
Designed and typeset by Dorcester Typesetting Group Ltd.

CONTENTS

What's Special About

GIRL TO GIRL

WOW! The girl world is great! Have you noticed? Girls are incredibly strong, resourceful, caring and insightful! Girls are bold and interesting and interested in the world around them. In other words, girls have a lot going for them! Not the least of which is their ability to make, keep and take care of their friends.

Have you and a friend ever shared a secret? Confessed your most private thoughts? Laughed out loud together? Cried on each other's shoulder? Girls just seem to naturally gravitate toward each other like some sort of cosmic force! They can't help themselves . . . they just need their pals to talk to, confide in, share with and have fun together. Do you know why? It's their nature! They're just naturally inclined to connect! And researchers are coming to see just how important that is to the happiness and well-being of girls everywhere.

Girl to Girl – Friends and You! is written for all the girls around the globe who have ever been touched by friendship. In it, you will find the voices of other girls – just like you! Girls have a lot to say about their friendships. In *Girl to Girl –Friends and You!* girls share their experiences with friends, the good, the bad and the ugly! From the ways they've been helped and the times they have felt cared for and supported by friends, to the situations when they've been confused or concerned about their friendships – hurt, they tell all. In this book, you will also read what girls have to share about their best friends, next-best friends, and boy friends (as opposed to boyfriends!). They confess their frustrations about the issue of popularity and the pain of being in a fight with a friend.

Readers will learn about what is important to girls, about their lives, and about their relationships with their friends. This book is for any girl who has ever wondered: What is a best friend? How do I know whether I can trust my friend? Can a boy really be a friend? Hear what the experts have to say, and what the ultimate experts – the girls themselves – have to say too!

So, this book is really an advice book based on the experience of hundreds of girls who have been willing to share with me what is happening with their friends. The girls you will meet in the pages of this book are real girls with real friends living real lives in real places. Some are from the United States and some are from the United Kingdom, Australia and elsewhere around the world. Hopefully, by hearing from so many girls, every girl will recognize what they are going through in their own lives, and know that they are not alone.

I hope reading this book will leave you feeling like you just had a great talk with a friend. And I hope you will be as inspired by the girls who share their lives in this book as I have been.

Anne Driscoll

GIRL TO GIRL

1

the
Real Deal

on
Being
Friends

Friends

I found I felt most happy when my friend asked me if we could be best friends. She made me feel special when she told me I was very pretty and very lovely and that I was perfect in every way. RACHEL, 12

I feel most happy when I am with my friends and we are all having fun. I feel like this because we are all together and enjoying ourselves. I feel saddest when I break up with my friends or we have an argument. I feel like this because they are a part of me and when we break up I feel like I lose a part of me. LAURA, 13

I am happiest when I'm with my best friend and my other friends. KAREN, 12

I think honesty is very important in a friendship. Without honesty, a friendship isn't much of a friendship. You also need to trust someone. You need to trust them so they don't tell your secrets. You need, to a certain extent, to be dependent on each other, for instance when they need a shoulder to cry on. A sense of humor I think helps with the friendship by making it stronger. KAYLEIGH, 13

I feel most happy when I am with my friends. I feel so happy because my friends are really nice and happy and we have a good laugh. EMMA, 12

The best thing about friendship is having someone with you all the time, no matter what happens. LAUREN, 12

Times when I feel the most happy are when I am with my friends, because I enjoy being with them and they're a great laugh. I like to hang around with my friends and go out. My favorite activitiy to share is going shopping. RAWINDER, 13

COLBY Age 10

Lives with: her mother, a college administrator, her dad, a consultant, and her sister, age 6

Best friend: Skyler

Pets: a rabbit

Favorite activities: "I have my own business making and selling perfumes. I love to decorate the bottles and make flyers."

Worst moments: breaking an ankle and another time having stitches

Feels happy: "When I get a good grade on a test and a good report from my parents after a parent/teacher conference night."

Enjoys: spending time with her family

Interests: soccer, softball, dance, shopping, sleepovers and having fun with friends

friends are

Best friends. Buddies. Confidants. Pals. Chums. Mates. It doesn't matter what you call them – girl to girl, friends are what count. Best friends or good friends. Pen pals or email buddies. Camp friends or playmates. The world of girls is populated with friendships of every kind. **And with good reason!**

Colby knows this – for sure! She has known the importance of friends for as long as she can remember. She's had friends as far back as nursery school – probably even before that. "You can have so much fun with your friends," explains Colby.

Girls especially understand this. Girls just seem to be driven to connect with one another. It's their special nature. Truly. Absolutely. Undoubtedly. Girls are born into the world with a strong desire to bond with others. When they're wee babies, scientists have found that they are entirely fascinated with the human face and totally turned on by connecting with other human beings. Their entire drive is to be in relationships with others, beginning with their parents and siblings.

As they grow and develop, those relationships enlarge to include others outside of the family. And guess what? Friendships are born! Maybe at a playgroup for toddlers. Perhaps at the playground on the swings. Or at the childcare center. Girls just want to connect! It's the most important thing in the world to girls! Researchers are coming to truly appreciate this aspect of girls' nature. While child experts have long known the enormous influence parents play in a girl's life, they are only now beginning to understand the extraordinary significance of girls' friendships. **Outside of family, friends are the most momentous relationships a girl will ever have!**

Colby, like many girls her age, takes her friendships pretty seriously. She spends a lot of time thinking about them, a lot of time caring for them and a lot of time maintaining them. She knows it's all time well spent. She loves going over to each other's houses, doing projects together, or watching a movie while sharing a bowl of macaroni and cheese. She enjoys her friends so much. It's

I feel most happy when I'm around all my friends because they make me feel so good. All my friends are good kids and really nice to everyone. LAUREN, 12

I feel most happy when I'm surrounded by more than one friend. I feel secure and all of us laugh together. SARAH, 12

My group of friends and I are a very humourous bunch. Mind you when I say friends I mean boys and girls! I love my friends because each is an individual and though I may not like every quality about them, I certainly still treasure their good sides and if I can do that, it makes life a lot simpler in the friends department! STEPHANIE, 13

I like to have lunch with my friends and gossip, talk, eat ice cream, ride bikes, play in the snow, bake, and paint our nails. My favorite activities I share are sports, such as soccer. BROOKE, 12

I always feel happy when I'm with my friends. They're very important. We talk about boys, what's happening in school – you know, girl stuff. My friends are very important because if you've got a problem, you can talk to them in confidence. I think trustworthiness and honesty are the most important qualities in a friendship. CHERYL, 12

The time I feel most happy is when I spend time letting loose with friends. I try to act loose as much as possible, but some of my friends don't always let loose. When I get them to, it makes me happy and it's fun to be around them. SHELLEY, 14

just the best feeling ever to be in the company of someone you care about – and someone who cares about you.

"I feel the saddest when I'm lonely because no one likes to be lonely," she explains.

Fortunately with so many girls out there in the world, there's no reason to stay lonely for long. Colby has found this out for herself . . . sometimes the hard way. When Colby was in kindergarten and first grade, she felt lonely – a lot. Very often at school recess, she found herself with no one to play with. You see, she REALLY wanted to become friends with a girl in her class named Skyler, but Skyler already had so many other friends. It just seemed to Colby that there was no place for her to fit in the group and at first, no one even seemed to notice that Colby *wanted* to join in. And worse still was the fact that some girls noticed, but didn't seem to care.

TRUE OR FALSE?

Having good friends and strong, supportive relationships will . . .

__ T __ F increase your lifespan

__ T __ F make you feel happier

__ T __ F strengthen your immune system

__ T __ F keep you healthier

__ T __ F boost your self-esteem

__ T __ F help you to become more
successful

__ T __ F reduce stress

__ T __ F lessen depression

__ T __ F prevent colds!

If you answered True to all of the above, then you understand the TRUE value of friends! Amazing as it seems, research scientists have found that friendships do more than add to your social life – friendships are an asset to your mental, physical and emotional life, as well.

"It's just that Skyler knew all these girls before and I wasn't the first friend she ever had," said Colby. "I couldn't fit in and I couldn't get to her because everyone else was talking to her. She really didn't notice me when she was around them. I'd say, 'Skyler, I have to tell you something' and she'd say to the other girls, 'I'll be back in a minute.' Sometimes they didn't want me around and I would try to say, 'Skyler' and they would turn their backs on me; they would keep talking to her even though they would have noticed me. They would ignore me and I would feel left out."

What could Colby do? Should she sulk and pout and hope that the girls would feel so bad they would ask her to join their group? Should she tell them off? Should she give up? Get angry? Tattletale? Cry? It was confusing. She felt confused – not to mention sad, hurt and angry.

Colby ended up trying different approaches. Some days, she would simply spend recess reading a book outside. Sometimes, if everyone was playing four-square, she would wait in line. Sometimes, she just didn't know what to do. "I did feel like I was not wanted at that time. I was just, like, walking around the playground because there was nothing else to do. I just tried to find a game I could play by myself," says Colby. On many days, she simply kept trying to do whatever she could to reach out to the group, to get the other girls to notice and accept her.

"It kind of hurt my feelings, although Skyler wouldn't know I would feel left out," remembers Colby. Finally, Colby decided to do a very bold and brave thing. She decided she would just talk to Skyler about the situation and be honest about her feelings.

"I decided I would ask her if she would come over and I would tell her how I felt and we would all work it out," says Colby.

And did it work out? Colby is pleased to report: yes, it did. Skyler is now her very best friend in the world. And that's not all. "Me and Skyler and Jessica and Ali are all friends. We're all friends now, but before I didn't fit in," says Colby.

COLBY'S TEN TIPS ON MAKING NEW FRIENDS

1. invite people over to your house to play after school

2. try to keep in contact with those you'd like to get to know better

3. invite others to play games with you

4. if they keep giving you the cold shoulder, then try to go to someone else who *will* be your friend

5. make yourself visible – go on the swings, watch others play basketball

6. make your own fun – play a game that others might want to join you in playing

7. be friendly – it's the best way to become a friend!

8. be persistent

9. be nice

10. be interested in them

This is what worked for Colby. Maybe it will work for you, too. Remember: It's not always easy making a new friend, but it's always worth it!

Friends are pretty special people, after all. Researchers have found that having friends is as important to a healthy, happy life as food, water and air! We need friends. We want friends. And, in turn, our friends need and want us. And isn't that a beautiful thing? What a wonderful bond between two human beings!

special

Who else will tell us 'you look awesome in that outfit' and really mean it? Who but a friend will listen patiently as we complain about the pile of homework we just suffered through? Who but a true-blue mate would help us figure out what to do with our hair? Our bothersome big sister? Our niggling self doubts?

But how do friends accomplish all that? How do friends help each other over the rough spots of their lives? How do they support each other? Cheer each other on? What is it that friends do together that is the glue that cements the friendship? They talk, of course! There are few things more comforting than a talk between friends. Having a friend with whom you can share your secrets, sadnesses, fears and triumphs is the most wonderful feeling in the world.

I am most happy when I'm with my friends as when I get home I have to be all grown-up and sensible and when I'm with my friends, we can really have a good laugh together. HANNAH, 12

It is very important for me to talk to my friends. We usually talk about boys, life, school, books, music and many other things. I think the qualities that are most important in a friendship are honesty because if you're not honest, then the person's not really your friend; trustworthiness because if you can't trust them, you can't tell them very much; dependability, because if you can't depend on them, you're on your own; and a sense of humor, because if you can't laugh with them, it won't be a very happy friendship. MARGOT, 12

I like to TALK, play outside, go to the mall, go to the movies, go over to each other's houses and do all sorts of fun stuff. Our favorite things to share are what we have been doing, playing games, listening to music, BOYS, and all sorts of fun activities. KELSEY, 12

I confide secrets in all of my friends . . . It's very important to talk to friends. We talk about school, tests, students and we talk about sports. Dependability and a sense of humor are the most important things in a friendship. BRITTANY, 12

Here is what is TOTALLY amazing and awesome about friendship:

You become more yourself by becoming more of a friend. Maybe that sounds a little silly, but it's true. As girls are joined together in friendship, they also discover their own individuality! We learn who we are, what matters to us, what we value, how we think – all by being a friend to someone else. Isn't that weird?

But, it's also very useful. Let's face it, growing up can be really confusing. It's a challenge, isn't it? Sometimes, growing up is incredibly exciting. It's all so fresh with possibilities. But on other occasions, it feels a little overwhelming. Figuring out who we are and who we want to be is made a lot more simple by having a friend on hand. In many ways, a friend can act as our own personal mirror, helping to reflect back our own image – who we are today and who we might grow to be. Girls need the connection of each other to grow in strength and health and happiness.

Colby and her best friend Skyler are so connected to each other they sometimes feel like sisters. Or maybe even twins. In fact, they used to dress alike. When you dress identically with your friend, it's a way to express – and show everyone else – just how close you and your friend truly are.

"It's kind of cool to dress as twins," says Colby. "All of a sudden one of us would be calling the other up. We'd call each other in the morning and say, 'You want to dress the same?' I guess it was a fun thing – a way too for other people to know we made up from a fight or we were friends."

I feel sad when someone important to me gets mad at me because I sometimes think that they won't like me anymore. ANNA, 9

I feel that if my friends don't accept me for what I am, then they can't be a real friend. LAURA, 13

I feel happy when I help people or even just make them laugh. It gives me a buzz because I think one of the most important things in life is to laugh, have fun and look on the bright side. I feel sad when I'm not included in things at school or when I say something without thinking and really hurt someone's feelings! STEPHANIE, 13

I feel happy when my friends and I get to be together and play with each other. I feel the saddest when I am lonely and no one is there to play with me. With my friends I like to play sports, do an art project, go on walks, and talk about school and friends. My friends and I usually talk about teachers and why we like or dislike them, boys, or activities that we like to do. LAURA, 10

I feel most happy when I'm out with my friends, if it's at the cinema or just round someone's house. I feel the saddest when I break up with my friends as I feel lonely and I can't have a good gossip with them. I have never stayed un-friends for more than three days because we just start talking again. KERRI, 12

Oddly enough, there was a time when the fact that they were wearing the same shoes got them into the biggest fight ever! Colby thinks it's silly now, even bizarre, but one time they got into a HUGE argument because they both had the same white sneakers with heels. (This happened at a time before they decided it was cool to dress alike.)

"I was at her house and I saw the sneakers out on the floor in her room. And I said, 'Oh I have those' and she said, 'you do?' I said 'yea,' and then she said, 'I got them first. Why did you get them Colby?' I told her, 'I go to the same shoe store as you, I didn't know you had them. I saw them and I liked them.' And she got all mad. She told the babysitter and so this whole thing started and the babysitter got involved. We sat on the couch and were both crying. We were mad at each other for about a week and we couldn't stand it. And then one day, at recess, I said,

'I'm really sorry' and she was like, 'I'm really sorry.'

And we made up until we fought about the next stupid thing."

The next stupid thing was never ever again about wearing the same clothes, though, because it was soon after that horrible fight that Colby and Skyler decided it was kind of fun to look like twins. That was awhile ago. "We don't dress up like twins anymore – now that we're in fifth grade; we're older and we have more homework – we don't have time to call each other and coordinate outfits. I don't know – we just don't want to do it anymore," explains Colby.

Colby finds it **SO** interesting how their friendship continues to grow and change over time – just as she and Skyler are growing and changing. Their friendship – so far – has been able to accommodate the changes. There are times, of course, when they might not necessarily agree, when there might be some conflict that disrupts their friendship, but they are learning ways to smooth over their differences and **keep their friendship going**. Colby and Skyler have a better understanding of each other and are more able to accept each other. They appreciate both the ways they are alike and the ways they are different.

Colby says, "We really don't fight very much. We just don't have anything to fight about. We're best friends. We've known each other all our lives. We respect each other – we don't get mad at each other. We accept each other. We just don't fight anymore. We just are alike – we shop in the same stores, we go over to each other's houses a lot, we don't really have anything else to fight about. We try to solve fights at the moment they happen with our babysitters and stuff. If that doesn't work, we kind of stay away for a couple of days to feel sorry and then we can't take it any more because we're really good friends. We respect each other.

We're just really nice to each other."

best friends

Besides her best friend Skyler, Colby has many other friends, too. There are the other girls she and Skyler hang around with, like Ali and Jessica. There are other girls at school that Colby plays with too. Then there are her out of school friends, like her best friend from camp. "We send letters to each other – we just really try to keep in touch with each other. We write to each other if something happens so we know what's going on, like when I broke my ankle and cut my hair," says Colby.

I think it is important to be able to talk to your friends. I talk about my family, problems, and lots of other interesting things. MANDEEP, 12

My friends and I play plays. Like acting out your favorite book or movie. We confide secrets about boys, our sisters, my brother, and Austin Powers. ROBIN, 11

When I used to have a lot of seizures, she accepted me as a friend and didn't make fun or anything. CODIE, 12

When my auntie died my friend totally understood because her mum had died. You know someone's a friend when they actually listen to you and you can trust them completely. JENNIFER, 12

"I'm really close with my coaches, I get to know them because my dad is my coach too. I have had teachers I've had really good relationships with, too."

Colby appreciates all the special friendships she's cultivated in her life. She enjoys showing those special people just how important they are to her. She might make a card for a friend or offer to stay after school to help her teacher clean up. It's important, Colby believes, to be nice to others. She also realizes that by taking care of your friends, you're taking care of your friendships. And there are few things more valuable to her than her friendships. Colby is not unlike

special people

other girls around the globe who value their relationships and take care to nurture and maintain them. Researchers have found that girls gain their sense of self-esteem in large part by how they gauge their ability to make and keep friends.

"I think kids can make themselves popular just by having good friends and by being a good friend," says Colby. "You make yourself popular because people want to be friends with you."

Are you a good friend? How do you make new friends? When can you trust someone to keep your secrets? How do you make up with your best friend? What do you do if you find out your friend was talking about you behind your back? Can a boy be a friend?

These are just some of the questions that will be considered by girls just like you. Hopefully, girl to girl, you will find common experiences that you've shared with your friends and in *Girl to Girl – Friends and You!*, you will gain more understanding of yourself, your friends and your friendships.

The girl world is
GREAT!

I think the most important qualities are honesty, trustworthiness, and someone who likes you the way you are. A friend should be able to keep secrets and tell the truth. They should not have to change the way you are. And they should not use you. It is very important to me that I am able to talk to my friends. We talk about problems that we are having and what we are doing later. RAWINDER, 13

When I am with friends, we go shopping, see movies, play sports or just hang out. we always do something that both of us like so that then we are both having fun. Sometimes in the summer we'll go swimming or go for walks. Even if we are just hanging around, it's still fun. ASHLEY, 13

All my closest friends like to act, sing and dance like I do. We also love to talk, paint our nails and play outside. I tell my closest friends things like boys that I like. ANNA, 9

HOW IMPORTANT ARE YOUR FRIENDSHIPS?

1. When you wake up on the weekend, your first impulse is to . . .

A. Go back to sleep.
B. Check out what your mother has planned for a family outing.
C. Call your best friend and figure out a plan for the day.

2. You've forgotten to bring home your math book, you . . .

A. Wonder how to explain why you didn't do your math homework to the teacher.
B. Ask your mother to take you back to the school to retrieve your book.
C. Call your friend and beg her to share her book!

3. You've made the soccer team and you immediately imagine . . .

A. What fun it will be to score a goal.
B. Your parents cheering you at a game!
C. Making lots of new friends.

4. You and your best friend have just gotten into a huge argument over the silliest thing . . .

A. You decide to forget about it and watch TV instead.
B. You complain to your mother about your friend's insensitivity.
C. You can't take being apart another minute and call her to talk things over.

5. You are having the worst "bad hair day" in the history of hairstyles!

A. You wear a hat!
B. You ask your mother to make an appointment for a makeover!
C. You call your friend to whine and then invite her over to fix your head!

If you answered mostly As, you are fairly independent.
If you answered mostly Bs, you depend on your family for support.
If you answered mostly Cs, you count on your friends to be there for you!

2 Best Friends

I have a best friend that I would die for. She is kind, understanding and thoughtful. I feel like we share a soul. ANNA, 9

My best friend is Anna. She's always got a smile on her face and she makes me laugh. I think it's hard to know when you've got a best friend, but when you've got one you know. Anna is the best thing I've got. She's always there for me. I can always trust her. CHERYL, 12

My best friend understands everything. She's nice and very friendly. SARAH, 12

I do have a best friend. She is my best friend because she's nice and I can trust her with anything. LAUREN, 12

I don't really have one best friend. I have four best friends. Gretchen is my best friend from school. We have known each other for a long time. We live on the same street and go over to each other's house a lot. Rossli is my best friend from hockey. We are very close friends. We have a lot of jokes to tell and we laugh a lot. My best friends that I have been with since I was little are Jameson and Tyler. They used to live across the street from me. Whenever we play with each other I'm always the only girl. I don't mind though. KELSEY, 12

I don't have any secrets, but if I did I would tell my friends. Not ordinary friends, just best friends. SARAH, 12

My best friend's name is Lindsay. Although sometimes we get on people's nerves, we always cheer each other up and have room for a laugh. BRITTANY, 12

JENNIFER Age 12

Lives with: her mother, a part-time heritage center guide, her father, a college student, and her 11-year-old sister

Interests: tap, jazz and ballet classes, singing lessons, going to the movies, swimming with her friends, having sleepovers

Future career: "I want to be a forensic scientist. I'm just really interested in the science. I really like it a lot; I'm quite good in it."

Friend philosophy: "It's important that you listen to one another, be there for each other and trust one another completely."

Most embarrassing moment: "When I had just started Year 7, I was sitting next to Natalie when I sneezed and everything came flying out of my nose. We just laughed about it."

There is a strong bond that exists between girlfriends.

It is undeniable. You only have to look around the playground or watch girls at the mall to see it. Girls walking side by side, giggling and whispering in each others' ears. Girls sitting together at McDonalds sharing fries and secrets. Girls trying on clothes for each other in The Gap dressing room. Yet what is this mysterious force that keeps girls connected invisibly? It's not simply love. Yes, we love our friends. But, friendship is more than feeling love for someone else. We love our pets, but we might not necessarily go shopping with them!

It seems, then, that there is some other force as strong as love, but different, that bonds girls to one another and keeps them connected. What is it? Understanding? Commitment? Respect? Loneliness? Could it be all of those things? Probably all that – and much, much more!

For Jennifer, she remembers that her friendship with her best friend Aimee began with a casual bit of friendliness that just **continued to grow deeper over time**. She and Aimee have been friends since they were 7 and Jennifer remembers the day in class when she first met Aimee. Jennifer was sitting at a table with her friends, a group she had known since they began nursery school together. Aimee, on the other hand, had come from another school and sat at Jennifer's table.

"She was on her own. She sat at our table and we started talking," said Jennifer. They ended up working together on a lesson and continued chatting with each other. Jennifer immediately liked Aimee. There was just something about her. She was kind and sweet. She was quiet and caring. Above all, she was really, really nice.

"She's very caring and she listens to you. It's hard to explain. She's not afraid to say things. She's always nice to you, listens to you and if you need help, like advice on school work or whatever, she's not afraid to offer it," explains Jennifer.

Of course, Jennifer has other friends as well. **Close, caring relationships** with other girls (and boys). In addition to her friendship with Aimee, she's very close to a girl a year younger than Jennifer who lives three doors down the street. It's a sisterly sort of relationship. Then there's the friendship she more recently started with another girl in school whom she finds funny, caring and sensitive. And then there's the other girl who Jennifer describes as "very gentle." Jennifer finds her to be someone who "really listens, not just nods." And Jennifer has friendships with two boys in her class with whom she and her friends sometimes go shopping and hang around. All of these relationships offer something unique and important to Jennifer, although she describes Aimee as her "very best friend."

Researchers believe that girls look toward each other to discover themselves. Girls' friendships, in a sense, act as mirrors. We look at each other to see if we see ourselves. Is she/am I nice? Are we both good sports? Kind? Sensitive to others? Do we laugh at the same things? Prefer the same ice cream?

I have a best friend. She is very sporty like me and she supports the same football team and we have much in common. She is my best friend because she was the first friend I made in secondary school and we have a lot in common and she is really nice. MANDEEP, 12

I have a best friend named Jessie. I have known her for a long time. She is my best friend because we can always talk to each other. We both understand each other and are always there for the other. We can tell each other secrets and know that the secret will never get out. Jessie and I both like doing soccer and dance, so we have a lot in common. ASHLEY, 13

Share the same fashion sense? Girls very often find their friendships offer amazing possibilities for self discovery. They learn about themselves from learning about their friends. Strange, huh?

So friendships are extraordinarily important to girls. They provide companionship, a shoulder to cry on, a friend to laugh with and a confidant to share life's troubles with. But they also provide girls with the chance to understand themselves better. Has a friend ever told you, "You are so patient." Or, "You are a good friend." Or, maybe, "You are **SO SILLY**!" These statements are a reflection of the way others see you and help you get a sense of your own self image. Just by talking things over with a friend, you may often discover some new fascinating and amazing thing about yourself and your personality! Isn't that totally awesome? Way cool.

Sometimes when several friends see themselves sharing a certain number of things in common, they might assume they also share, in a sense, an identity. For example, they might think, 'we are the girls who all absolutely **LOVE** the Backstreet Boys.' Or 'we are as close as twins because we all wear the same style clothes.' If you think about it, one of the main tasks of childhood is growing up, and one of the main tasks of growing up is figuring out who we are. Friendships serve girls well, then, in helping them discover who they are and identify who they want to become.

Friendships are also the first relationships girls make outside of family. It is through those relationships that girls begin to form an idea and image of themselves as separate and different from their families. Have you ever had a secret you would share only with a friend? That kind of private thing you might not share with your mother, father, sister or brother? Sharing secrets with a friend is something almost every girl does!

It's totally normal!

Not to mention fun! By disclosing some secret thing with a best friend, girls are able to feel the safety of sharing something they're not sure about, or are embarrassed about, or are confused by – all within the safety of a supportive, accepting friendship. Girls are able to disclose their inner selves to their best friends and be accepted.

And that is so cool!

> I do confide secrets with my best friends that I can't tell anyone else.
> CAROLYNE, 12
>
> I only tell my best friend my secrets. EMMA, 12
>
> I do confide secrets with my best friend which I do not confide with my other friends. And I tell them things I don't share with anyone else. We talk about problems we are having. RAWINDER, 13

> I tell many secrets to my friends – mainly only one person because it's not a secret if everyone knows. I tell them things like who I like, I often ask for advice on matters such as when I have an argument with someone. STEPHANIE, 13
>
> My best friend is very funny and it's fun to be around her. She is my best friend because we have a lot in common. I tell only my best friends secrets that I won't tell anyone else. I tell them who I have a crush on and I know that they won't tell anyone because they can trust me with that kind of secret. LAURA, 10

Being with girlfriends also give girls the chance to gain insight into the complex relationships we count on to support us. For example, when girls are playing house together, they're not just practicing the routine of keeping a house, they're also play acting what it means to be a spouse, raise children, have friends. The friendships girls develop provide a window into the wonderful world of relationships and relating! Let's face it, it takes practice and skill to be a good friend, a caring companion, and a sensitive pal!

Over time, Jennifer and Aimee came to know each other better and their friendship deepened. The two were good friends at school, and sometimes, on occasion, Aimee would come by Jennifer's house. There was a little wrinkle in the relationship, however; at one point, Aimee had become friends with another girl and Jennifer didn't always like the way Claire was treating Aimee. Jennifer felt protective of Aimee and concerned she might get hurt, but little did Jennifer realize Aimee's relationship with Claire was the least of their worries.

That year, when the girls were eight, something unexpected and tragic shattered the ordinariness of their lives, something that both Aimee and Jennifer took for granted: Aimee's mother died. Aimee knew her mother was sick, but didn't realize how horribly ill she really was. Her mother's death shook her to the core because Aimee hadn't really expected it. Under the circumstances, Aimee needed a sympathetic ear and comforting touch. And quite often, she turned to Jennifer.

"It was me she talked to because she felt she could trust me more. She knew her mother had been ill for quite a while but no one told her how ill she was so it was quite a shock. She thought she just went in the hospital for a short time. We were kind of sad. We didn't know things

We all talk about boys and makeup and that sort of thing and it's a laugh. But the more private stuff I find really hard to talk about. Most of the time I keep it a secret but if I can't do that then I only tell my best friends who won't let it out.
KERRI, 12

sympathetic ear

33

like that could happen," explains Jennifer, who recalls first hearing about the death of Aimee's mother one day at school.

"One day Aimee took the day off from school. First of all we didn't believe it – the teachers told us. We were all really nice to Aimee, although we didn't really know what to say to her. She was quite shy, she didn't say too much. She talked about what happened and she didn't know what was going to happen – she was a bit upset that no one told her."

In ways small and great, Aimee's loss brought Aimee and Jennifer closer together. Jennifer could never replace the relationship Aimee had with her mother, but Jennifer could provide her own measure of warmth, comfort, support and steadiness to Aimee at a time when she really needed it. Friends do that for one another. No one is protected from disappointment or discomfort in life, but having a friend to share the pain does help take some of the sting out of it.

"I was pleased she chose me to talk to because at the time I thought she was friends with Claire. But even in spite of that, Aimee considered me a close friend," remembers Jennifer.

For reasons Jennifer is not really sure of, Aimee came to rely on

When my daddy was gone she understood because her daddy was gone too!
ROBIN, 11

I do have a best friend. She's in my class. She's a few months younger, and she sits with me and hangs around with me. She is my best friend because she is an honest, kind and caring person and someone to talk to. She keeps secrets and doesn't tell people. Also she doesn't use people. **RAWINDER, 13**

I do have a best friend. We have been best friends since first grade. We can tell each other anything and we can cheer each other when we are sad. I tell my best friend a lot of stuff that other people don't know. **CODIE, 12**

Jennifer, confiding in her about what she was going through. Although Jennifer had never experienced such a distressing loss and couldn't imagine what it would be like to one day find yourself a motherless child, she knew instinctively that Aimee needed her to be there for her. And that, Jennifer knew, she could comfortably do. Jennifer knew how to listen, care and be sympathetic. And she was willing to support Aimee through such a difficult time. Jennifer was eager to do whatever she could to help her feel better.

Going through rough times together often strengthens a friendship. This was true for Aimee and Jennifer. The trust they sensed in one another grew and the closeness they felt deepened as well. Jennifer wants to be there for her friend in good times and bad, and the same can be said for Aimee. Aimee has been a source of support and comfort for Jennifer when she's had troubles, too. "When my auntie died Aimee totally understood," says Jennifer. As the two girls have grown, so has their relationship. By the time they were nine or ten, they began doing things outside of school, as well. Their relationship had graduated to a whole new level of friendship, which is very often what happens between girls as their connections deepen and grow.

"Aimee used to come around for tea every now and then. Then when we were 9 or 10, we were older and we felt we could do other things. We were more responsible. We'd go swimming, do things together without our parents, or we'd go shopping. Like we went shopping yesterday for Christmas presents. She is so nosy! I was trying to buy her Christmas presents and she's saying, 'what are you buying?'

Aimee and Jennifer are now attending separate schools, but it hasn't harmed their friendship at all. Researchers have found, for example, that best friends may not see each other for long periods of time and yet the friendship remains intact. Very often, neither time nor distance come between best friends, rather what is important is that friends believe that there is still ready affection

36

and acceptance of each other. Therefore, no matter how far apart they are, the friendship remains healthy and strong.

"She doesn't go to the same school but we still see each other. She goes to ballet with me on Wednesdays and we do loads of things together. We go to the cinema or swimming or go out in larger groups with some of the boys or other friends. When we go shopping, its normally just the two of us," says Jennifer.

Girls often **admire** their friends greatly. They like the way they look, think, act or talk. Sometimes they appreciate traits in their friends because they see them also in themselves, but sometimes they adore a friend's personality because they see their friend possessing some trait they wish they had. Occasionally, admiration can get twisted into envy, which often times complicates the feelings of friendship. Some girls admit that they can get jealous of their best friends (or of their best friends' other friends), but learning to manage these conflicting and complicated feelings is all part of growing up.

It's all part of being a friend, too.

Fortunately, for Jennifer and Aimee there haven't been many times when there's been that sort of envy dividing them. Instead, they've come to truly appreciate each other's special nature.

DO YOU DEPEND

1. When I am lonely, I . . .

> A. Call my best friend.
> B. Try to get over it myself.
> C. Tell my mother.

2. A girl at school called me a total loser. I . . .

> A. Ask my friend if she thinks I am a total loser.
> B. Cry myself to sleep that night.
> C. Complain to my mother that a girl is picking on me.

3. A boy likes me but I am not sure I like him. I . . .

> A. Stay up all night at a sleepover gossiping about him with my best friend.
> B. Make a list of his good and bad points to help me decide.
> C. Ask my brother what he thinks of him.

4. I am worried that I am too fat. I . . .

    A. Ask my best friend's opinion of my appearance.

    B. Decide to starve myself until I am as thin as Kate Moss.

    C. Beg my mother to take me to a diet doctor.

5. I am so worried I am not going to pass a huge test scheduled for the next day. I . . .

    A. Invite my best friend over to study together.

    B. Get totally stressed out and nearly have a nervous breakdown!

    C. Tell my mother that school is so unfair.

If you answered mostly As, you are getting the hang of hanging out with a best friend. You are learning what it means to give and take in a relationship.

If you answered mostly Bs, you may be very self reliant, but perhaps feel alone. You could use the benefits of a best friend.

If you answered mostly Cs, you rely on your family for support, but may want to branch out to share more with a best friend.

"By the time we were 9 or 10, we could talk about anything . . . whatever, whether it was having a problem, or about doing school work together or going to the library to do our homework if we had projects. We'd talk about school, people at school, teachers at school and things out of school, like music and things – normal kids' stuff. We talked about everyday things. I would tell her things like if I had a problem, although it was never as big as what happened to her, but she listened to me anyway. She made me feel comfortable sharing with her," says Jennifer.

"We'd also talk about boys and other things like if you're having a problem with people at school – which by the time you get home, it's not important, but when you're in school, it's the major thing."

In fact, Aimee and Jennifer never seem to run out of things to talk about. And they are so happy to have each other to discuss all the minute details of their lives. "I think it's very important to have friends you can trust. I have cousins I can talk to, too, but I still like talking to Aimee. When we're sitting in our bedroom together or on the phone we can talk about anything. You can talk easier with your friend and in a different way than you can talk to your family. Besides, if you're having a problem with your family then you can't talk to them, but you can talk to your friend and she'll understand."

40

With a best friend you can be whoever and whatever you want to be and still be accepted. You can be outrageously silly and she won't tease you – she'll probably join the fun, too. In fact, there might be some occasions when you and your friends act like first class citizens of Goofy Nation. For Jennifer, she remembers when Aimee had her 11th birthday, and Jennifer, Aimee and another friend went to the cinema together. At some point, as a joke, they stuck a bucket of popcorn on Jennifer's head. Later, they went to the McDonalds, and Aimee accidentally knocked the milkshake down Jennifer's front and the lid came off. Then, the other friend spilled ketchup and fries onto Jennifer's lap and while they were walking home, stuck a napkin under her hairband.

"My mum said, 'Look at you . . . What have you been doing?' It was fun; we still

still be accepted

enduring friendship

talk about that now and we still laugh about it now," explains Jennifer.

It may sound like some corny cliché, but being best friends means sharing the good times and the bad. It means knowing when to laugh together and when to share a box of Kleenex tissues. It means offering a pat on the back when a friend needs support and a slap on the back when you share a belly laugh!

Even now, Jennifer says there are times when Aimee finds herself thinking about her mother and feeling that loss all over again. "Because we were friends when that happened, it means I understand when she wants to talk about it now, because even now when she's 12, she needs to talk about it every now and again," says Jennifer.

There are those special moments when Jennifer realizes she has something very special with Aimee. She and Aimee share an enduring friendship that keeps them connected to each other in a unique and remarkable way. She felt that deep attachment one day when Aimee, Jennifer and Jennifer's mother were out shopping for a party dress, for a school dance, for Jennifer. They found a great dress for Jennifer but Aimee also spotted a velvet dress she really liked for herself, although she didn't have the money to buy it. "My mother bought her that dress," says Jennifer. Of course, the dance was that much more outstanding because they had had such a special time preparing for it together.

Will they remain best friends *forever*?

Who knows? Undoubtedly as they grow and change and meet new friends, their friendship will be challenged, and probably change, in ways they can probably not predict. Already, Jennifer has seen Aimee change some as she has developed new relationships with other girls at her new school. For one thing, she has experimented with bleaching her hair.

"I told her she never would have done this before – you don't have to stick your head in a bottle of bleach to be accepted. I think she did it because she's so unsure of what she can do; she's unsure of herself. She is tempted to do just what everyone else does so she can have some friends," says Jennifer, who hopes this is just a phase her friend is going through.

But Jennifer is committed to her friendship with Aimee and still makes sure they get together every Saturday. "She listens to all my problems despite having had a very troublesome life. We do everything together and are *always* on the phone!!" says Jennifer.

> " I think that it is important that you can trust all of your friends completely. I think that honesty is important and so is a sense of humor. "

My best friend is Megan. She's a very loyal friend and nice and funny and caring and we are blood sisters. My relationships with my other friends is nowhere near as good as with my best friend. Me and Megan never really see any of our other friends except school and we practically see each other every day and never get tired of each other. I don't believe in more than one best friend because if you get in a fight, then you'll be on someone's side and not the other. And if you start to like one more than the other then that's not a best friend. KAREN, 12

Since starting high school my best friend and I have kind of drifted away. From her I have learned, though, that you should be nice and caring to friends especially cause you never know when they're not going to be there. STEPHANIE, 13

My best friend has the same interests as me and we go everywhere together. We've just recently had a falling-out but we're going to make up on Monday. I just know it! She's my best friend because we just get on so well. HANNAH, 12

I tell my best friend everything. There are a few more friends I tell most things but most of my friends don't know everything about me. LAURA, 13

I do not believe in best friends. I don't think it is very fair to treat one friend better than the other. I treat all my friends the same. So you could say that all my friends are my best friends. RACHEL, 12

WHAT KIND OF BEST FRIEND ARE YOU?

Check off all that apply.

____ I would never betray my best friend

____ I always check-in with her first before I make plans

____ I am loyal to her

____ I always try to be sensitive to her feelings

____ I am trustworthy

____ I always save her a place at lunch, a seat at the movies, etc.

____ I talk to her at least once a day

____ I would never gossip about her to anyone

____ I admire her

____ I appreciate her friendship

____ I respect her

The more you've checked off, the more mindful you are as a friend. Learning to be a good friend is like learning any other skill. It takes practice and commitment.

WHAT KIND OF BEST FRIEND IS YOUR BEST FRIEND?

Check off all that apply.

___ She would never betray me

___ She always checks-in with me before she makes plans

___ She is loyal to me

___ She always tries to be sensitive to my feelings

___ She is trustworthy

___ She always saves me a place at lunch

___ She talks to me at least once a day

___ She would never gossip about me to anyone

___ She admires me

___ She appreciates my friendship

___ She respects me

The more items you have checked off, the luckier you are to have found such an awesome best friend!

Now, how do your two lists match up? If they match up pretty well, then it seems you've found a great match in a best friend!!!

Next Best Friends

At school we like to help at the library. But sometimes we just sit on a bench and eat lunch and have a good laugh. Outside school I love to go to the cinema with my friends and watch a scary film. We scream and squeeze each other's arms. SARAH, 12

Well one of my other friends and I were really close, but just recently, I've noticed that she has got a really bad attitude. She gives us all a laugh but she also gets on our nerves. Another one of my close friends is really loud and always shouting. But all my friends have good points about them. KERRI, 12

I got one more best friend. She's always nice and I am so nice to her, she said I'm like a sister!!! But sometimes, she can be a pain because she likes to hug people too much. ROBIN, 11

The qualities that I think are most important in a good friendship are honesty, trustworthiness so that I can tell them secrets, a sense of humor so that I can tell a joke and they won't take it seriously, and personality. I have a lot of friends that play sports and I like that a lot. *KELSEY, 12*

All my friends have awesome qualities. The most important qualities to me are honesty because I don't like people who lie; trustworthiness because you need to be trusted and to trust friends; they have to have a sense of humor because if you ask anyone they will tell you I love to laugh and sometimes I do it too much; and they also have to be nice. *LAUREN, 12*

I don't have a best friend. I feel that everyone is my friend, but I have numerous best friends. Those are the people I like and enjoy being with. *BROOKE, 12*

I share secrets with my best friend. With my other friends it depends on how secret the secret is. We share secrets about who we love and things like that. *KAYLEIGH, 13*

MARGOT Age 12

Lives with: foster mother, an art teacher, foster father, a head-teacher, and two foster sisters, ages 11 and 6

Best Friends: Maggie, Judy and Sarah

Favorite activity: READING! Margot reads 2 or 3 books a week in the summer and 1 or 2 books during the school year. "I just like how whatever you think about when you're reading, you're just in the book's world. I always picture it happening in my head – like watching a movie only more vivid and interesting, I find."

Favorite musician/singer/performer: Backstreet Boys and Sarah McLachlan

Most Treasured Time: visits with her mom and dad, and, time spent with friends, too. "I do not get to see my parents much, so when I do get to see them we usually have a really good time and I treasure it. I don't get to see one of my friends much, so when I do see her, I usually have a really good time also."

Also enjoys: swimming, tennis, school sports

Margot doesn't have a best friend. She has three "best friends". Some might think that is a contradiction. How can three people earn the title of "best friend"? Well, Margot couldn't choose a single best friend because her three closest friends each offer her something different, yet equally important.

"I tell my best friends my thoughts, feelings, who I like, things like that. I feel like they're my own diary that I talk to instead of write to. The things I tell my best friends I would not feel comfortable sharing with my other friends," says Margot.

"When we were little, we were like, 'yeah someone to play with,' but when we were older, we got to trusting each other with secrets and stuff. And I do think as we got older, our friendship got stronger. Mostly we just talk – with all of them, I talk. Once in a while, we play some kind of board game or watch a movie, but really the talking is what counts most. They're really important to me now. I always have someone to talk to."

Margot's gone through some difficult times in her life. This past year has been one filled with changes and challenges. Because of her parents' problems in caring for her, she moved from home to live with a foster family for awhile. Margot says her foster family has been "kind, supportive, helpful, everything you need. I am glad to have them." They have offered a stable home for a time, although she also hopes to someday return home to live with her parents

My friends are kind and very caring. They are very, very funny. They are just lovely. They are very good listeners. RACHEL, 12

I tell some of my friends secrets. I don't tell all my firends my secrets because I know how easy it is for things to slip. So I tell my friends who I can really trust with my secrets. I do tell them things that I don't share with anyone else. Some things would be about other friends, boys, teachers or family. ASHLEY, 13

One of the main topics in our group at school is who likes who but while that's gossip, I believe you should be able to share problems that are troubling you, like you may be feeling left out, or you might be fighting with your parents. It could be even that you feel threatened. STEPHANIE, 13

I have lots of other friends. Some of them are my best friends but not all of them. I have three best friends in school. They all like to talk which I like because I like to listen! I think a relationship works well when one likes talking and the other likes listening. KAYLEIGH, 13

I do have other "best friends." They are my best friends because they are all nice and trustworthy. My favorite things to do with friends is to shop, hang out, play sports and listen to music. It's very important to talk to friends because everyone needs one good friend to tell stuff to. With my friends we talk about our favorite music, who we like, what we are doing and stuff like that. LAUREN, 12

again. But in the meantime, her three best friends have become especially important to her in this time of change. They are a consistent presence in her life at a time when everything seems changeable. Margot has known her three best friends since she was quite young. In turn, they know her well and understand her "best." And although Margot considers each of them her "best friend" that doesn't necessarily make them best friends with each other.

"Judy I met in kindergarten at school, I met Maggie at first grade in school, and I met Sarah in preschool. They all know each other but they're not the best of friends," says Margot.

Margot feels such a strong bond and deep connection with her friends. She counts on each of them for support, depends on each of them for understanding, and relies on each of them for kindness and caring. In that way, her three "best friends" are all the same, equal in that they each offer her comfort, insight, support and help.

"They're sympathetic. I think they understand me," says Margot. But in some ways, Margot recognizes that each friend is unique and likewise, each friendship is different too.

"I live with Maggie. She knows all about what's happened to

me. I knew her as a friend before I moved in with her family. On the weekends, I usually do things with Maggie and I'll do some things with Judy. Me and Maggie will do things with Sarah. And me and Judy will also do things – I'll go sleep over at her house, for example."

In fact, Margot has a **distinct relationship to each friend** and each friend has a **differing relationship to each other**. "They know each other – they don't hate each other. I don't think its very difficult to be friends with them all because I have my own time together with them separately. Maggie – I live with her; I see Judy and I see Sarah. I don't find it hard to keep the friendships going," explains Margot.

"Maggie is my foster sister and she's in my same class, my same grade, in the same homeroom. We have different rooms, but living with her family has brought me a little closer to her. I tell her most things. We tell each other more because we're around each other so much."

But what about Sarah and Judy? Do they get jealous? Feel competitive? Do they ever worry that Margot is **TOO** close to Maggie. After all, Margot and Maggie live together. They may have their own rooms but they also live under the same roof and how is a friend to compete with **THAT KIND** of closeness? But Margot is clear that each of her friendships are different and each offers her something equally special. And Margot is discovering she has many needs which different friends are able to meet.

"With Judy I like everything. I think about what is unique about myself and I'll talk to Judy about it and she'll say, 'Oh my God – I do that too!' We have a lot in common. She's easy to talk to and I just think she's a nice person. We usually talk and we'll probably rent a movie and watch it. That's about it. We used to stay up really late. Now we don't – we usually stay up no later than 12. We used to stay up until 3 a.m. almost every weekend," says Margot.

> **" With Sarah, we usually talk and if I go over there, Maggie comes too. I like Sarah because she's like really funny. She can make you laugh all the time. She's seems to understand me. She wouldn't laugh at me if I told her something serious. She's a really fun person to hang around with. "**

VHAT KIND OF QUALITIES

Rate them from 1 to 15
(1 is least important; 15 is most)

____ trustworthy

____ friendly

____ sense of humor

____ sensitive

____ able to keep a
secret

____ a good listener

____ a good talker
(willing to share)

____ pretty

____ strong self-esteem

____ nice

____ smart

____ cool

____ positive attitude

____ strong

____ courageous

**This should give you a profile of the
kind of friends you most desire!**

From the moment of birth, we are born into an exclusive relationship: baby and mother. And from then on, we spend our lives learning to make room for other people as well. Sharing the people we love or feel close with is not simple, though, or easy. And when it comes to friendships, sharing can be very, very complicated, indeed. Figuring out who are our friends and to what extent we can count on them – and they on us – can be fraught with conflict, or not. We are often wondering: How important am I to my friends? Do they really care about me? What do I mean to them?

My friends and I don't fight. We get along together a lot. Some of my friends have gotten in fights but I have never gotten into it because I want to stay friends with them so I just stay out of the fight that is going on. KELSEY, 12

My other friends are nice. Most of my friends have a lot in common but some of my friends hate each other. My friends are people I can talk to. CODIE, 12

I don't have other best friends. I have lots of special friends but only one best friend. I feel like I am alone if I'm arguing with my friends. All my friends and family are very special to me. LAURA, 13

Likewise, your friends may be wondering the very same about you! Trying to establish your place within the context of your friends may be a challenge – especially since it can be constantly changing. You know the saying about three being a crowd? When there are more than two friends involved, girls can feel like they are jockeying for position and like a horse race, if they don't come in first then they're **TOTAL** losers! It's hard not to feel competitive.

"I don't think it's a problem. Maggie and Sarah are good friends. Judy and Sarah aren't very good friends and Judy and Maggie aren't very good friends. They're friends, but not good friends like I am with them," Margot tries to explain.

But wait, that's really confusing.

How **does** Margot keep all these relationships straight? How **does** she maintain her friendships without hurting anyone's (or everyone's) feelings? How **can** Margot make Maggie, Judy and Sarah each feel reassured and secure that they are a "best friend?" Taking care with friends and taking care of friendships can be a very complicated business. But thankfully, girls have some natural skills at nurturing their relationships. They are very keen observers of social situations so they generally have a handle about who is friends with whom. In addition, they are practiced at relationship skills. When it comes to relating, they're pretty much experts. Girls want to be nice, take care of others and be sensitive to the feelings of their friends. The care and keeping of relationships are important to girls and they spend an incredible amount of time and energy using these nurturing skills, learning what it means to be a friend, and understanding how to uphold their share of the friendship.

very complicated

This is the great task of being a girl:

To figure out their relationships.
To learn how to balance their needs with
the needs of others.
To understand how to trust, how much to
trust and whom to trust.
To achieve a balance between closeness
and connection and separateness
and autonomy.

Girls are continually weighing their desire to be nice to their friends with their wish to be nice to themselves because sometimes those two hopes conflict with one another. And generally speaking, girls don't want to make anyone unhappy. They would rather everybody be content! Conflict is not easy for girls since when there is a rupture between friends, it usually means someone is going to get hurt. And the more friends you have, there is more likelihood that that's going to happen!

Have you ever had the experience of feeling really close to a friend? Someone you think is special and cool and nice and funny and trustworthy? And then, out of the blue, she gets mad, or ignores you, or doesn't bother to wait for you after school? If that has happened to you, then you understand how friendships may sometimes appear to be rock solid, but then seem to evaporate into thin air! How can you be sure you can count on anything, if you can't count on your friend? And just when you're convinced that you've found a friend that's as dependable as sunrise, something happens and your friendship falls apart like a month-old cookie.

We need our friendships. When we're with our friends, we are not alone! When we have company, we have companionship. When we share ourselves with friends, we give and get back so much! Our friendships protect us against loneliness. They give us a sense of who we are. They help us manage our feelings and understand our lives. And having many friends, gives us more

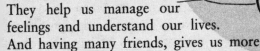

variety, more richness, more flavor. We may absolutely love chocolate chip ice cream, but if that was the only dessert we could ever eat night after night, it might lose some of its appeal.

THINK ABOUT IT . . .

IF WE HAVE LOTS OF FRIENDS:

- We never have to sit at lunch alone!

- We never have to cry by ourselves!

- We always have someone to call!

So Margot is happy to have the three best friends she does. She appreciates each of them for their own specialness and their different ways of supporting her. Her friends are there for her all the time, although that does not mean she wants to be with her friends 24-hours a day either! Sometimes she just wants to be by herself, to withdraw into the comfort of her own space. It's a way to relax. It's the time of day when she doesn't have to always be thinking about the intricacies of her friendships and the dynamics of keeping everyone's feelings in mind. She can just be thinking about her own feelings, an exercise everyone needs in their lives.

"Well, when I get home, I have some time in my room alone where I hang out and read or do stuff alone. Maggie and I might talk some times but I usually have time when I do my own thing and have some time when I can be alone at the end of the day. My friends and I might talk in school some also, but I usually have some time to myself. We usually give each other space to do stuff.

Afterwards, I feel a little better . . . not so overwhelmed. I go in my room, do homework and after that I usually just read because I love to read, I think, listen to music."

There are many other "friends" that Margot sees during the course of the day, as well. Since Margot has just started attending this school, there are opportunities to meet new people and make new friends. "We usually sit together at lunch with some other girls. I don't know them as well so they're not like best friends yet," says Margot. "I have many other friends besides my best friends that I can talk to. I cannot tell them as much as I can tell my best friends but I can tell them a lot."

In the meantime, she treasures the friends she has right now and takes comfort in the fact that they are building a friendship over time.

"Having the same friends for a long time shows you – you can see – how they change and you know them better. You know them pretty well and they know a lot about you, too, since you've known them for so many years. I think you can have a really good friendship with someone you've just met too, but it just so happens that I've known my friends for awhile."

building a friendship

1. You've been asked to go to the mall by one close friend, but your other close friend said she was also going to call you to make plans . . .

> **A.** You tell your friend you can't wait to go to the mall, your favorite store is having a huge sale!
>
> **B.** You tell her you'd love to go to the mall, but you have to check in with your other friend first. Then you decide what you'd rather do for the day and who'd you rather spend time with.
>
> **C.** You tell your friend you'd already sort of made plans with your other friend, and would it be okay if she came along too?

2. Your friend starts talking about another friend of yours . . .

> **A.** You agree with every bad thing she says about her.
>
> **B.** You let her have her say, then tell her your other friend is not that bad.
>
> **C.** You tell her you don't really want to talk about someone you care about like that.

3. You and your other two friends have always been an awesome threesome, but lately, you've noticed the other two spending more time together without you . . .

> **A.** You get angry, decide to ditch them and find other friends to hang with instead.

B. You feel a little bit hurt, but decide not to say anything.

C. You are worried about your friendship and ask them if there is something wrong.

4. A girl from the most popular group in school approaches you, telling you that you have a few admirers from her group who'd like you to join them to go to the movies . . .

A. You can't believe your lucky stars and jump at the chance to be part of the in-crowd!

B. You say, YES! Then think up some excuse to break plans with your other friends.

C. As excited as you are, you tell her you have plans with your other friends, could they come along too?

If you answered mostly As, then you are seriously challenged by having more than one friend at once. You need to learn how to manage multiple relationships in a way that's satisfying to you and fair to your friends.

If you answered mostly Bs, you are getting the hang of juggling multiple friendships in mid-air! Keep practicing and you'll master it!

If you answered mostly Cs, you value each of your unique friendships and work hard to maintain them all – even when they might conflict with one another. You will never be lonely.

4

FRIENDS THAT ARE

BOYS

I have a lot of good friendships with be__ play on a boy's hockey team and a__ boys just treat me like another playe__ the team. I talk with a few of them on__ Internet. I also talk with some boys tha__ from my school on the Internet. Tyler i__ best friend who is a boy. I go over to his house a lot. KELSEY__

I have a lot of friends that are boys. Some of my friends have "boyfrie__ which I think, at 12, is ridiculous. If you have a boyfriend y__ supposedly "cool" but I disagree with this statement. BROOKE, 12

In primary school my relationship with boys was the same as__ relationship with girls. I had a lot of boy friends and girl frie__ MANDEEP, 12

I have friends that are boys. I don't have boyfriends. SARAH, 12

ALISON Age 9

Lives with: her mother, a seamstress, and her dad, a business owner, a sister, 6, and brother, 3

Interests: acting, singing, Irish step dancing, skiing, swimming. "I've been skiing since age 3. I've been swimming and exploring the water all my life – my mom dunked me into the water when I was one."

Musical interests: playing the recorder. "I practice everyday. I play Greensleeves and I can play a lot of things. I'm good with my ear – music comes naturally to me. I can sit down and figure out the first few measures of a song on the piano if I hear somebody sing out."

Favorite Books: currently reading "God's Little Acre" and has read all three Harry Potter books.

Hobbies: collects dolls from all over the world and has dolls from South America, Russia, France, Ireland and England.

Pet Peeve: "Sometimes I get annoyed by my sister, but I'm trying to control that. We're actually really good friends and I often get bored when she's not around."

Have you ever had a boy friend? Not a boyfriend, but a boy friend? A boy who you pal around with? A boy who is a great playmate? A boy who is fun to talk to? A boy whose company you enjoy?

Believe it or not, these boys exist!

And many girls report actually knowing them. Some girls grow up thinking of boys as the enemy or as some strange alien form. These girls may come to believe that boys are something best avoided because who else but a freakazoid boy would steal your place in the lunch line, annoy you with weird burping noises and feel absolutely confident you enjoy seeing him show off?

It is true that boys may have some habits you find, at best, curious and at worst, offensive. But boys aren't necessarily nasty, they're just, well . . . different. And many girls have found that once they get beyond the blustering, boastful bravado, boys can actually be really nice guys. And – would you believe – good friends!

Alison has discovered this for herself. "I have three very close friends and I like each of them for different reasons. One of them is a boy," she confesses, although some of her friends don't understand; they wonder if she isn't a bit crazy to have a boy as a friend. But, that doesn't bother Alison a bit. She really likes Jeremy and can't imagine life without him.

Jeremy makes her existence a whole lot more interesting, not to mention

FUN!

I think that as you progress in grade levels you start to find boys that are just as nice and trustworthy as girls. Lots of times it's easier to talk to girls, but it's cool to hang around with boys, especially if you can relate to them. Boys are cool to talk to about sports, and to laugh with and have as friends. LAUREN, 12

I have many friends that are boys. I hang out with boys and girls. I really don't think that it matters if you hang out with boys and girls both. They are all my friends anyway. I have known a lot of boys for so many years and some of them are still my friends. I would say that many of my good friends are boys. Although many are girls, also. ASHLEY, 13

I have a very good relationship with the boys at school. In fact, I treat them the same as my girlfriends! I think in every circle of friends, at times, girls may have a bit of an argument and a few people get left out for a while. That's why I think it's important to have both so you have a change of scene every so often. STEPHANIE, 13

I have a friend named Andrew who I have known for as long as I can remember. We used to live next door to one another. Other than that I believe that boy/girl relationships at my age – 12 – is ridiculous. BRITTANY, 12

Everyday they're inventing some new brilliant scheme together. One day, they might pretend to be detectives, spying on their sisters. Or another day, they might be talking in some secret code language they've made up together. Or perhaps, they become playwrights for the day and perform a dramatic production they've collaborated on.

Whatever mischief or mad plan they engage in, Alison says it's guaranteed to be fun when Jeremy is involved. "We're really close. He is really creative and he always has something adventurous in mind. What I really like about him is that some of my friends are afraid to do something that might be breaking the rules somewhat. I like to have fun – thoroughly and completely – and he isn't afraid to do that. Everytime I come over, he is inventing something. His inventions rarely work but sometimes they do," says Alison.

For example, one time Alison arrived at Jeremy's house only to discover he was creating his own play dough recipe, mixing tissue paper, water and flour, which Jeremy discovered could be molded into shapes, dried and painted. "We would mold them into plates – although they didn't really look like plates, but we would have a lot of fun anyway, even if it didn't work out," remembers Alison.

When she and Jeremy are together, Alison just never knows what will happen next. Both Jeremy and Alison love reading detective stories and one of their favorite games is playing detectives in which they make up plots that have to be solved. It might mean they have to use their brain power to solve a mystery or it might mean they have to sneak out a first floor window to avoid being discovered. Whatever game they play, role they take or plan they follow, it's likely to include unexpected turns and interesting twists. And it's always fun, says Alison.

"My parents and his parents call us the mischief makers. We are always reading detective books and we want to be spies and detectives, so we pack little backpacks and run around the house pretending our dog is a monster. We turn the house upside down. We kind of like bug our little sisters and spy on our parents. We do daring things like climbing out windows, although we've never done anything dangerous. We've dreamed of it. We've sat around and pretended we're detectives who do dangerous things. One time we jumped from a window and we've also swung from a rope to the ground."

Why do Alison and Jeremy share this close relationship? Who knows? Alison says they've known each other all their lives because their parents have been friends forever. But that doesn't explain why Alison and Jeremy connected, or how they have managed to maintain this friendship over time and distance. It could be some sort of weird, strange destiny thing, maybe.

"Jeremy is three days older than me. Actually he was supposed to be born on March 5 and I was supposed to be born on March 2 but his birthday is March 2 and mine is March 5. Everybody thinks we're cosmic twins or something. We have the exact same nose, exact same freckles in the same places, the same hair color and the same eye color. When we were babies, people would say, 'Oh . . . cute twins.' My mom would say, 'They're not really

twins. In fact, they're not even related,' says Alison. "Actually we still look alike."

Whether they're really cosmic twins or just down-to-earth pals, their relationship is not really that surprising because it has many of the same elements as any friendship between girls. Just like Alison and her girl friends, for example, Alison and Jeremy like one another, enjoy each other's company, appreciate each other's personality, share many interests, and have come to trust and accept each other.

But, let's face it.

Boys ARE different.

Have you noticed? They're obviously different in physical ways. But, they're also different in less visible ways too. Consider this: child experts now believe that the nature of boys is unlike that of girls. Boys want to show off about how strong and separate and in control they are, while girls, on the other hand are driven to be connected and in relationship with others. This may explain why boys are always challenging, wrestling or racing each other to show off their stamina, speed or strength, while researchers have found that girls tend to prefer cooperative games (such as playing house or dolls) or talking to one another, where the goal is to interact and connect.

Here's something else **REALLY** interesting – and weird. Boys and girls are born with the same capacity to relate to other human beings. That means baby boys and girls are all equally social creatures. All babies' survival, for example, depends on their relationships with their mothers, first of all, as well as their other caregivers. But then something happens to boys about the age of 4 or 5. Around that time, they get the idea from books, television, music and movies that relationships aren't supposed to be that important to them. It's okay for boys to have friends, for example, but friends are people you do things with, not talk to! Boys learn that "real boys" are supposed to be tough, strong, cool and unemotional. Boys are not, for example, supposed to cry. This puts boys in an awful predicament. They may want to be real friends connecting on an emotional level but feel like they can't afford to show that softer side or else they'll be accused of being a sissy, wuss or girly-boy.

Isn't that too bad?

But, there is hope. There seems to be a greater understanding that boys and girls both need relationships! Many parents and child experts are coming to see that boys who try to live up to some unrealistically tough boy code are not really satisfying their need to have the close, warm and satisfying relationships with their peers to the degree that they might. There is a small but growing awareness that boys have . . .

. . . **GULP!??!!** . . .

FEELINGS TOO! Even the boys themselves are coming to see it – although they may not admit this in public. But Alison has noticed, for example, that while the other kids who know about her friendship with Jeremy might be curious (and there was a time before when they would occasionally get teased that they had crushes on each other), no one these days seems to be particularly bothered by it. "The boys know about our friendship and they're perfectly fine with it," says Alison.

Believe it or not, regardless of whatever anyone thinks, some boys manage to find a way to maintain friendships of all kinds, to **ACTUALLY GET CLOSE TO ANOTHER HUMAN BEING** without jeopardizing their reputation as a boy. Alison says that Jeremy, for example, is considered a "really cool boy." The fact that he hangs out with a girl hasn't really affected his friendships with other boys. Jeremy has a lot of guy friends with whom he rollerblades or hangs out at the park. So, his friendship with Alison expresses one aspect of a very complicated personality with many complex needs.

"He acts so much different when he's with me than when he's doing boy things and acting like a boy. The other boys think he's so cool. He rollerblades, he bikes, he hangs out at the park. When he's with them, you don't even see the kid I see when I'm playing with him," says Alison.

"But then again, whenever I'm with a girl it's so different. When I'm with a girl, I need to be a girl – fully a girl. And when I'm with him, I'm just a fun person. Sometimes we run into each other at the park and when we see each other it's funny."

Having a friendship with a boy can offer girls a chance to get to know boys in a totally different and entirely casual way without all the seriousness and stickiness of being "boyfriend and girlfriend." It's **SO** much less complicated!

WHAT DO YOU LOOK FOR IN A FRIENDSHIP WITH A BOY?

Rate these in order of importance from 1 to 15.

___ someone to listen to you

___ someone who cares about you

___ someone to have fun with

___ someone who is brave

___ someone who is dependable

___ someone who is loyal

___ someone who is trustworthy

___ someone who is funny

___ someone who understands you

___ someone to do things with

___ someone who is adventurous

___ someone who shows an interest in you

___ someone who you share the same interests with

___ someone who will look out for you

This should give you a profile of what kind of guy friendship you want and need!

More

girls than ever are finding it's easier to become friends with a boy these days. For example, the fact that **SO** many more girls are playing sports now gives girls and boys much more in common. The playing field is literally a common ground for girls and boys. They have more to talk about. They have more mutual interests. They have more shared experiences. And as a result, many girls and boys are finding they have much greater understanding and respect for one another.

But does this mean that only girls who play sports can be friends with boys?

No way!

Playing sports may make it easier to strike up a conversation with a boy, but it certainly doesn't mean it's the only way to win a guy's friendship! Some boys may enjoy becoming friends with girls because it gives them a chance to explore a different side of their personality than they get to show with other guys. The same is true for girls. By becoming friends with a boy, girls have a chance to challenge themselves in entirely new ways. And very often, striking up a friendship with a boy can be as easy as saying, hello!

How to be friends with a boy . . .

☐ Take an interest in what he does.

☐ Invite him to go roller blading, biking or hang out at the park.

☐ Ask him to work on a school project or study together.

☐ Organize a party, barbecue, get-together, or outing with him, his friends and yours.

☐ Email him.

☐ Smile, say hi, be nice and friendly. That's the best way to begin any friendship!

Does this mean that you'll find your friendships with boys the same as your friendships with girls? Probably not. Of course every boy is different, so it's impossible to generalize, but chances are you will notice some ways that your friendship with a boy differs from those with girls. Alison has spent a lot of time thinking about this in her own situation.

"He's my, like, friend. I play with him a lot and I always have fun. I'm comfortable talking to him about things at home and family, but things like friendships with other girls and girl things, I talk to my other friends about . . . That is different because he's a boy. It's a very different experience being friends with a boy. A boy would never admit he's sad. Jeremy cried when his pet died but a girl would still be crying the next day. He's a little bit less social. We talk about fun things but I couldn't talk to him about really anything that has to do with a girl. I could mention things to him and he'd be understanding but I wouldn't really feel that comfortable having a long discussion with him about how I had a fight with a friend the other day. When I'm with him I'm not really the same as when I'm with my girl friends," says Alison. "When he's with the guys and I'm with the girls, we each have two sides of ourselves."

"Sometimes when I'm with my girl friends, we'll sit in the room and talk about boys we like. I could never do that with Jeremy if my life depended on it. If I have a problem, I would be more likely to turn to one of them instead of him. They would just understand me better – it's just that he's a boy," explains Alison. "When I'm with my girl friends, we do hair, put makeup on, dress up. I have a lot of friends that are girls and we sometimes put on tapes. One of us will judge the other two as to who is the best rock star. Like we put on a Britney Spears tape and pretend we are Britney Spears."

> The point is that whether Alison is playing detective with Jeremy or playing Britney Spears rock concert with her girl friends. she's still having fun!

Who could be bored with such a diverse group of friends? Certainly not Alison.

Alison gets a chance to understand herself better through her friendships with both girls and boys. She's also had an opportunity to get to know boys better through her long-standing friendship with Jeremy.

"I figured out that boys tend to not want to show anyone they actually cry or have feelings. I figured out they actually do have feelings even though they don't show it. When they do let them out, it's bigger than girls because they don't let them out very often. We've been around each other when he's gotten really, really sad and emotional, like when his cat died. He's sympathetic when anything happens to me. I realize boys actually have feelings, but they just don't want to let them out. I don't know why – they're not any different."

And so, Alison continues to enjoy her friendship with Jeremy. She hopes they continue to remain good buddies as they grow up.

I like boys a lot! I have friends that are boys. In fact a really, really GOOD friend of mine is a boy. CODIE, 12

I don't know very many boys that are my friends because I find a lot of them immature and hard to talk to. There are some boys I think would be OK to have as friends, but I don't see them very much. MARGOT, 12

I had a really good friend that was a boy and then we had a fight and I've given up on boys! We girls can get along without them! CHERYL, 12

I love having guys as friends. All my life I've had good guy friends. They are caring and helpful, without being involved. They always make me laugh and I enjoy being around them especially when I'm having friend troubles. My closest boy friends (two words) are Matt, Eric, Brent, Scott, Kris and Chris. I can talk to them and still have fun with them. They are my friends unconditionally. SHELLEY, 14

She continues to be amazed by him and curious about his perspective on things.

"I sometimes wonder how he's so confident. Even though I'm really confident, he always says what's on his mind no matter what it is. I don't mean he'd insult somebody. I just mean he's different. I'm saying that **without boys and girls**, I think life would be pretty boring," says Alison.

HOW WELL DO YOU KNOW BOYS?

Check off what you think is true or false

1. Most boys would rather stay in and talk than go out and play. __ T __ F

2. If a boy doesn't tell you he likes you, he probably doesn't. __ T __ F

3. All boys think girls have cooties. __ T __ F

4. Most boys enjoy the various sounds their bodies can produce. __ T __ F

5. To show affection, boys are unlikely to hug one another but they will wrestle. __ T __ F

6. Just because a boy acts tough, does not mean he has no heart. __ T __ F

7. Most boys like to be on the move. They don't like to stay still for long. __ T __ F

8. Boys' friendships are really important to them. __ T __ F

---

1. FALSE. *Boys generally are very active creatures who prefer doing to talking!*

2. FALSE. *Boys may think and feel a lot of things they don't necessarily express. Many boys keep much of their most important feelings bottled up inside.*

3. FALSE. *A good number of enlightened boys realize girls are cootie-free.*

4. TRUE. *Boys can become fixated on the noises they can emit out of their nose, mouth, armpits and other body parts.*

5. TRUE. *Many boys feel they can't hug a good friend because they'll be accused of being a sissy (or worse). Weird as it may seem, wrestling is considered acceptable physical contact, however.*

6. TRUE. *Boys often do not show on the outside the warm feelings they might have inside.*

7. TRUE. *Have you ever watched them play at recess? They are constantly moving targets!*

8. TRUE. *This may come as a shock, but boys have feelings – including strong feelings of friendship!*

5 OTHER BUDDIES

I have many other friends on sports teams and in school. We comfort each other and motivate one another. BRITTANY, 12

I have some very close friends from camp. These friends I spend 3½ weeks with each summer. I have become very close to them and I tell them basically everything. My friends from camp are some of my best friends. I also have a friend who lives in France. I met her three years ago and I haven't seen her since. We do write letters and keep in touch. We have a good relationship because we tell each other many things about our lives. ASHLEY, 13

Another friendship that was important to me was with my teacher Greg and I will never forget it. He was smart, funny and had high expectations. ANNA, 9

I have an email buddy living in Canada. We write to and fro and it's great to hear what happens over there. I also have a penpal. He lives in Kiama, Australia and he is extremely important to me because we used to live next door to each other. Then he moved. I didn't want to let go, so we write and tell jokes to each other. STEPHANIE, 13

MARISA Age 13

Lives with: her mom, a writer, her dad, a probation officer, her sister, 15, and her brother, 10

Favorite pastimes: basketball, softball, Playstation, instant messaging friends

Other interests: hanging around, going to the mall, shopping, movies, boys

Best Friend: "I don't have one best friend, I have six best friends."

Most important thing in a friendship: "I just want an honest answer. I want them to tell the truth – whatever their opinion is."

Pet Peeve: being wrong

Favorite thing to do: laugh

Marisa feels really lucky. She has a nice family, lives in a great neighborhood with lots of kids in it, enjoys her school, plays on several sport teams and has **many pals** she relies on for friendship and fun. She counts at least six "best friends," although she also has other friends too. Truthfully, she would have a hard time picking out one "best friend," although some of her best friends she feels closer to than others for various reasons.

Marisa is happy to be surrounded by so many friends and so much friendship. She loves talking to her friends on the phone, emailing them on America Online or hanging out together at each other's houses. There isn't a day that goes by when she's not been in contact with at least one of her best friends and usually many of them or often all of them! It makes her feel great that she has the comfort of so much companionship. She almost never feels alone or lonely. Even so, Marisa also knows that she has other friendships that don't fall into the category of "best friend" but she considers them to be really important nonetheless!

Let's face it, there's no **one way** to be a friend.

Friends come in all sizes and shapes and so do friendships!

It's really cool how many ways there are to make friends. Think about it: Perhaps you have friends you have made through playing sports. These are teammates who have stuck by you, come wins or losses! Or maybe you have made friends at camp with girls able to fill that empty place you felt inside during those first homesick hours away from your family for the first time! And, then again,

I have a friendship with my soccer coach because he helps me learn different techniques. I think of him as a friend. Also, I think of my sister Ashley as a friend because she has all the same qualities as a friend. I can trust her, I can rely on her and she is honest with me. LAURA, 10

I have a good friendship with a few of my teachers. If I had a problem I would find it easy to tell them. KAYLEIGH, 13

I have lots of email buddies. We met on a chat room and I really enjoy typing to them. My auntie is pen pal and I am really close to her. I tell her everything, almost. SARAH, 12

there might be other people with whom you've developed a deep, caring relationship because they've been your teacher, teammate, coach, neighbor or babysitter. Isn't that totally awesome – how many friends you can have in your life?

Friendship can be found in all kinds of relationships. After all, what is a friend? Someone who cares about you, is attentive to your feelings and concerns, listens to you, helps and supports you. There are many people who might provide all that caring and concern, although they might not be what you would consider traditional best friends.

Marisa discovered this for herself last summer when her softball team won the state championship and she went to the regional playoffs. Her whole team traveled by bus hundreds of miles and were placed with host families. The only problem was, the team was split up so one or two girls were assigned to live with a different host family. The whole idea made Marisa a little nervous.

Who would she be living with?

Would it be totally weird sharing meals with someone you'd never laid eyes on before?

What if she didn't like the food? The bed? The family?

What would she do?

Understandably, she was a little apprehensive when she arrived at the home of the family to whom she'd been assigned. But she soon discovered she had little to fear. Jenny, the 12-year-old girl who was part of the family, immediately made her feel comfortable and at home. The two girls hit it off right away.

"She was the same age. I shared a room with her. She was really nice. She made me feel welcome. She just like talked; she wasn't shy. She told me about herself. She slept on the floor and I slept on her bed. She gave up her bed and she was going to sleep in her sister's room because her sister was at camp but she decided to sleep on the floor so she could be with me," says Marisa.

The instant sleepover turned into an instant friendship.

"We talked about what our schools were like and what our teachers were like. She had a different accent than me. It was hotter there than where I live and there were more farms and fewer people than where I live, but we found out we had a lot in common anyway. We both liked softball and basketball. We both loved AOL instant messaging. We both liked TV, the same foods like chocolate, ice cream, french fries. We had ice cream every night. We'd make sundaes together wtih lots of chocolate sprinkles and hot fudge. **Most of all she was nice."**

Marisa's team didn't make it to the next level of final playoffs, but she did find a friend in the days she spent there. When it came time to go, she and Jenny exchanged email addresses and real addresses too. Jenny gave Marisa a photograph and Marisa promised to send Jenny one in return. Marisa found it easy to find friendship in spite of their differences and in spite of the distance. Sometimes sports is an easy bridge between girls or occasionally, it's the circumstances of being away from home, a stranger in a strange land looking for companionship and comfort.

WHERE DO YOU FIND FRIENDS?

Check off all the places you have found friends . . .

___ school
___ sports
___ neighborhood
___ camp
___ dance class
___ music lessons
___ theater group
___ art class
___ singing lessons
___ after school clubs or activities
___ through other friends
___ email
___ pen pals
___ other ways

There are so many places to find friends, it's amazing!

This was the case for Marisa last summer when she went away to camp for the very first time. Her older sister had been to overnight camp already and she had told Marisa what it was like. Marisa felt a little prepared, but then again, she didn't know exactly what the experience would hold for her. **Would she like the food? Would she be lonely? Would she be**

scared to be in the middle of the woods? Would she die of bug bites? Would she meet any new friends? And of all her fears, the concern over her social standing was the one that plagued her the most. After all, what fun is hiking, boating, archery, campfire songs and talent show skits if you don't have any friends to enjoy them with?

"This was my first time away from home. I was nervous at first because I didn't know what to expect. I was just getting settled in and we had our swim test. I was late getting there so I didn't have a chance to talk to anybody. Then after the swim test – which I passed – we went back to the cabin and that's when I met people. I introduced myself. I introduced myself to four people. They were talking to people I knew. I liked them right away because they were nice. They were friendly. We'd always sit together and talk. And we picked classes that we'd be together in. Like when we had to pick what activities we'd do, we picked the same thing in the same order, like Project Adventure, canoeing and water games. They were a lot of fun and we laughed a lot together. We'd eat together and we'd sleep together in the same cabin. We'd talk all day long and stay up later than we were supposed to and talk. Sometimes we would get in trouble with the counselors."

That nervous stomach – that feeling that suggested her insides were cramping up big time – disappeared as soon as she knew she had a friendly face she could count on. In fact, she had found four new friends. "Carolyn – she's nice, she's funny. Mary – she's really nice. She's like timid and she's really sweet. She's shy around other people. Sydney – she's wicked-nice and she's really, really funny. Dana – she's easy to get to know and friendly. I thought I was going to miss home but I didn't because I had all these friends. It was because of them that I decided next year I wanted to come back for two weeks," says Marisa, who emails her camp friends often or talks to them online.

Occasionally, friendships can crop up in places you least expect them to grow. Like mushrooms, they sprout overnight. Marisa, for example, could have never predicted the friendships she has found through her sports participation. Take her friends Mary and Jackie. Mary and Jackie both come from a different town miles away from her own. It just so happens they were all thrown together on the same basketball team and became teammates. Then that teammate relationship grew into something more deep and lasting – a true friendship.

"Mary plays forward and I play forward, so we both play the same position and are out there together on the wings. We have to pass to each other and we play well together. We practice that together and then we execute it in games. I feel like we know what we're doing and that contributes to the team. We talk to each other on the bench. We talk about the game and we joke," says Marisa.

"Jackie – she plays guard underneath the basket. She's nice. We talk about the game and we laugh together and stuff. It's nice to be on the same team together. We never talk to each other out of practice but it's nice to have friends on the team, and especially make new friends I would't know otherwise.

Marisa has come to appreciate all the different kinds of friendships you can have – each offering something unique. **It makes her feel rich in relationships.**

"I know I always have someone to depend on. I know I can have someone to relate to so I never have to feel lonely or by myself. I have a lot of friends. I'm always busy because I always like to keep in touch with them. I do a lot of different activities in my life and it's nice to know there's always somebody there no matter what I'm doing or where I am. I'm an open person and enjoy meeting new people all the time. Because I consider myself a friendly person and interested in other people, relationships are very important to me. I need friends. I learn about myself through other people. I think it's important to have friends because I don't want to be lonely and end up depressed."

It's **true** girls are very social creatures. Their relationships are the central focus of their lives and

My neighbor is one of my good friends. I also am her babysitter. I have long conversations with her and enjoy talking with her and hearing her input on things. BROOKE, 12

I have a pen pal in Australia. She's 12 and called Roshell. I get letters every three months. We send lots of pages of writing. CHERYL, 12

I have many friendships because of being on a skating team. I meet many people who I wouldn't have known if not for the team. I also have a penpal who lives in Maine who is really cool. My pen pal and my friends on the team are nice, funny, cool and trustworthy. LAUREN, 12

their friendships are the central focus of all their relationships. Girls want to experience the diversity of friendships that are possible. Girls hope to gain a greater understanding of themselves and others through their many unique friendships. They find kinship wherever they go, whatever they do.

As Marisa says,

" *Friends are important because they help me and I help them.* "

True or False?

Check off whether you agree or disagree with the following statements

___ **T** ___ **F** I believe friendships are worth working at

___ **T** ___ **F** I find my friendships very satisfying

___ **T** ___ **F** I have a variety of friendships

___ **T** ___ **F** I value my many friendships

___ **T** ___ **F** I am always looking to make new friends

___ **T** ___ **F** I consider myself a "friendly" person

___ **T** ___ **F** I am willing to make the first move in starting a friendship

___ **T** ___ **F** I am open to different kinds of friendships

___ **T** ___ **F** I realize that every friendship offers something different

If you checked 1 – 3 statements as true, you are cautious when it comes to friendship. Perhaps you should be a little bit more adventurous!

If you checked 4 – 6 statements as true, you are coming to see the true value of friendship!

If you checked 7 or more statements as true, then you are rich in friendship!

Does Being **Popular** Mean You Have a Lot of **6**

FRIENDS?

What makes someone popular should be because they are kind, helpful, caring and understanding. But in my class, I think the popular people are bossy, selfish, loud and annoying. LAURA, 13

What makes someone popular is they have lots of friends and are kind, pretty, athletic, etc. I know a popular friend who is so mean but still is popular and has little dogs that drool everytime they see her and stick to her like glue, even though she can turn on them at any point. BROOKE, 12

If someone is popular at our school, they're usually rich for some reason. They're also pretty and very domineering and when I say that I mean they stand up for what they believe. STEPHANIE, 13

I think that having the most friends and looks are what makes someone popular. RAWINDER, 13

I feel the saddest when I am excluded. This really makes me feel sad because I feel like nobody likes me. A time I felt this way was when a lot of my friends were going to a movie and they didn't invite me. Then the next day they were all talking about how much fun they'd had. They really excluded me even if they didn't know they were. ASHLEY, 13

SHELLEY Age 14

Lives with: her mom, an engineering statistics professor, and her dad, an engineer

Best friend: she has many close friends, but the closest is Brittany, who picks her up when she's down.

The best thing about her best friend: "We would both put our necks in the noose if it would save the other. She accepts me as I am and will always stand by me (and I, her)."

Favorite subject: "I don't really have one. I like classes that I don't like the subject, but I have so many friends in it, it's fun."

Feels great: when she's hiking in the mountains

Plays: flute, piano and school soccer

Favorite pastime: "I love, I love, I love to write books. I'm writing a book which doesn't have a name, but it's a take off on Sleeping Beauty. I have a journal in which I write ideas for the book."

Imagine you are

THE MOST POPULAR GIRL IN YOUR SCHOOL!

Everyone loves you, adores you, wishes they were you! When you get to school there is a rush of other girls to greet you. They jostle each other to walk with you to class. You are the girl others most aspire to be. You are **WONDERFUL**, aren't you? Isn't that what being popular means? That you're the most wonderful girl there is?

Who hasn't dreamed of being popular? What girl hasn't wished to be the one everyone wants to sit next to at lunch? Who wouldn't want to be surrounded by scores of adoring friends? Isn't popularity the most important thing in the world to a girl? Doesn't being popular prove how great you are? Or, wait a minute . . . does it really prove any of that, at all?

Shelley has been on both sides of the popularity divide and she has many interesting things to say about what it means to be popular – or not! She's been in the in-crowd and she's been an outsider, as well. And she's learned a lot from being both "in" and "out." She now understands both the appeal of being popular and the falacy of it. She now knows that **NOT** being popular can sometimes have its advantages, as well.

"I've kind of grown so I don't really care if I'm popular or not whereas when I was younger, I loved to have everybody surrounding me. I've taken the opinion that if they don't like me,

Being popular should mean having lots of friends but at our school it's not. At our school you're popular if you wear American Eagle or Abercrombie clothes. You end up being judged on what you wear instead of who you are. LAUREN, 12

What makes someone popular is that she is pretty, has a good looking boyfriend, etc. MANDEEP, 12

In my school, someone is popular if they are boy crazy and have friends. I think someone should be popular because they are nice. BRITTANY, 12

Sometimes someone is popular because she is pretty and sometimes it's because she's nice. People at my school think I am popular because I try to be helpful and kind. ANNA, 9

You're popular when you are confident. Then you get lots of friends. I think I'm fairly popular because I'm friends with everybody and I'm quite confident. KAYLEIGH, 13

then that's okay. I'm not going to suck up to have that extra friend – it's their choice," says Shelley.

"I'm open to new friends all the time, but I don't try really hard. If they want to talk to me, I'll talk to them. If it's just the two of us, then we can talk, but I'm not going to try really hard to get in the popular group. You have your really good friends, no matter, and why risk losing that to get a glimpse of the popular lifestyle?"

Up through third grade, there was no such thing as "popularity" at her school. She was enrolled at the time at a small private school where everyone knew each other and were friends. Then she switched schools and attended a public school and it was there she got her first glimpse of "being popular." Classes were larger and with more students and more possible friendships to make, some girls just seemed to be more popular. These girls had more friends, more admiration, more status. And, Shelley could see that they were considered more cool.

"At my first school, the whole time I was friends with everybody. The school was pretty small and everybody knew everybody, so popularity didn't really matter. You were friends with everybody no matter who you were. I moved to public school in the 4th grade and started to discover the cliques, who was popular and who wasn't, and I was trying to discover what makes them that way," says Shelley.

Shelley approached this new phenomena with the curiousity of a scientist. She wondered: what makes certain girls "popular"? And like any scientist, Shelley did her research thoroughly. She watched the kids carefully at the school playground, made mental notes of who seemed to have the most friends, and collected evidence of why. Do you know what she found out? At her school in fourth grade, the girls who were most popular were the ones who could play four-square the best! Isn't that interesting? That a playground game could determine who was socially desirable and who was less so. Shelley figured if she wanted to be accepted and fit in,

accepted

she should learn to play four-square well, although she was never better than a middling player. It didn't really bother her too much, though.

The following year, Shelley was equally curious about whether the same set of unspoken, but still understood, rules of popularity would apply. And she discovered a change. In fifth grade, it wasn't the girls who could play four-square that were the most popular. The social scene had shifted completely! Now it was whoever could play kickball the best was most popular. Weird, huh? But no matter how hard Shelley tried, when it came time for the team captains to pick their players, Shelley was always mid-list. She didn't mind terribly, though. She assured herself that while she might not have been Miss Popularity, she had a **lot of good friends** she could count on and she figured that's what counted most.

In the fifth grade, as everyone was getting ready to switch schools and go onto junior high, appearing confident seemed to add to one's popularity standing. Shelley remembers, "Things started to change and confidence became a big thing. If they could talk to anyone or if they could hold a conversation with anyone and they weren't afraid to be around new people, that was good. Being able to adapt, make new friends, and not be scared of getting new friends became important."

It was about that time, in fifth grade, that Shelley herself made the bold move to run for student council president.

"In fifth grade, I started to become more popular. I ran for student council president in fifth grade. I had people outside my little group of friends who

I think mostly everyone can be popular in one way if they just show it. I think people are popular if they have a lot of friends, are nice, athletic and other things. I sort of think I'm popular. I think this because I have a lot of nice friends. KELSEY, 12

I have never really thought about being popular but I have many friends that like me. BROOKE, 12

I don't know what makes someone popular. I think it's because they act really big and everyone likes it. CHERYL, 12

I think people are popular because they are loud and outgoing. I don't think I am popular because I am shy and I like to keep my ideas to myself. RACHEL, 12

What makes someone popular is if the people in the grade like them. You get popular by being daring and everyone liking you. SARAH, 12

liked me, so . . . I hadn't run against anyone but it gave people the idea that I wasn't afraid, that I was confident. The idea to run came fom my dad. I wasn't going to run for president, at all. And looking back, I could see I was a real preppy person who went for good grades, did all my homework, studied for hours for every test – I pretty much was a worry wort about grades and most people like that don't become very popular, so I have no idea how that happened."

By sixth grade, there was a new school with many new students coming from other schools. The social scene changed

YET AGAIN!

Shelley still had her same old group of friends from her previous school and made only one new friend. She took her time watching everyone, getting a sense of who was who and what was what. By seventh grade, her growing confidence gave her the courage to speak out about things she felt strongly about. Her passionate convictions were noticed by others – including members of the most popular group.

passionate convictions

"People accepted me but they were always my close friends, so I started to branch out and let people know how I felt about things. I was very opinionated and I still am, saying this is not fair, or I don't accept this. There's a group of people who are really popular at our school right now, and, for some reason they liked the way I voiced my opinion. They came to me and said, 'I had this big conversation with my best friend about how I admire you so much. We really like the way you voice your opinion and how you handle your school work,'" says Shelley.

SHE'S SO POPULAR!!!!

Test your knowledge about what it means to be popular.

1. Whether you are popular or not is extremely important in determining your longterm happiness in the future. __ T __ F

2. The most popular kids are always the most happy kids. __ T __ F

3. It is worth it to do whatever it takes to be popular. __ T __ F

4. The most poular kids are always the nicest kids with the most friends. __ T __ F

5. Popularity is the most important thing in school. __ T __ F

1. False. Being popular in school is unlikely to be a significant factor in whether you achieve happiness in life. Whether or not you like yourself is far more important than if others like you and see you as popular.

2. False. Very often, the most popular kids are unhappy because they don't feel confident that people really like them for themselves and accept them. They often feel driven to live up to an unrealistic standard of beauty, niceness, etc.

3. False. It is never worth it to compromise your values, safety or sense of self-worth to achieve an arbitrary status such as popularity.

4. False. Sometimes the most popular kids are the nicest kids with the most friends, but sometimes they are mean-spirited, conniving, manipulative and unkind! Amazingly, they have achieved status in spite of their dark side.

5. False. Learning, enjoying school, spending time with friends is the most important thing in school.

If you answered false to all of the above, then you know the fallacies of popularity!

"It was a pretty big surprise when they said, 'Yeah we want to hang out with you more.' That was like that last week of 7th grade and I didn't talk to them over the summer, so it pretty much was leaving the door open to me to go into their group. I would like them to accept me and pretty much mold together, but I am also pretty much of a package deal – if they don't accept my friends, I'm not going to try my hardest to be in their group. I don't want to lose my friends I have now. Whenever they ask me to come with them, to go trick or treating or to the mall, I say, 'Can I bring this person or that person too?' That way, they can get to know my other friends too."

Now when Shelley looks back, she can see how arbitrary it is who is considered popular and who isn't.

> **It is just so weird.** Everything was weird then and it's still so weird. It is pretty much luck of the draw and if you're nice to people. Confidence is one thing and some use it for something good, like to strike up a conversation with someone who is sad and lonely.
>
> That gives you more popularity than if you use that confidence to abuse or tease people or make people feel inferior because someday someone is going to stand up to you and your confidence is going to go down the drain. You're tearing down somebody's confidence to stabilize yours so you're probably not that confident after all. **"**

Shelley has seen girls who are willing to compromise too much in order to achieve status. Researchers know that girls are under enormous social pressure to "be like" popular girls and to "be liked" by popular girls. This kind of peer pressure can make a girl feel like she has to trade on her beliefs or her friends in order to get the reward of popularity. What is so strange is that sometimes popularity, which seems so all-important and enviable, is as hard to catch and hold onto as a snowflake. Shelley believes "catching" popularity can be an amazingly arbitrary – and perhaps even meaningless – achievement. It doesn't really mean what a lot of girls think it means. It won't necessarily make a girl happier, more attractive or more content. And yet, oddly, it seems so desirable!

Shelley's advice to anyone perplexed about popularity:

- Take some time to observe how people act, what makes them act that way and what draws people to them.

- Don't be concerned about your popularity because people who are popular rise and fall. Someone will be popular one year and won't be the next.

- Stay true to yourself and don't change so someone will take notice. If you stay who you are, that may be the way to popularity!

- Remember that you don't need to be popular to be happy!

Many girls have the mistaken idea that if they were popular, that would be the end of all their problems. They'd never have to worry again! But this is **SO NOT TRUE!** Very often, the girls who are the most envied in the school, are also the most miserable too! Sometimes a girl who is popular feels trapped. She thinks that since everyone thinks she's perfect, nobody sees the real her. Nobody knows that there are times when she, too, feels ugly or insecure. That she suffers with zits just like everyone else. That's the really strange thing about popularity: Being popular doesn't really make you any better than anyone else. Everyone has challenges, worries, concerns and weaknesses. Even the most popular girl in the world!

When it comes right down to it, being well-liked is very nice. We all want to be appreciated. But having to live up to unrealistic standards or arbitrary expectations can be a horrible trap. And far too often, popularity can put pressure on girls to do not-so-nice things to prove they're **IN** and others are **OUT!** So achieving popularity might exact a cost that outweighs what it's worth!

"I've seen people who have had really good friends and the popular people decide to adopt them into the group," says Shelley. "They decide to adopt them, but not their friends. So they end up losing their really close friends and if they get into a fight with the popular group, then they're alone. When their popularity streak ran out, they didn't have anyone. I wouldn't want to risk that for being popular for a short period of time. They pretty much have to ask for forgiveness from their old friends, say, 'I'm sorry I deserted you' and make it up to them. Either that or find a whole new group of people to adopt them into their group of friends."

Instead, Shelley has become a leader of her own group. She likes to think of this group as the nice group who makes room for anybody. "There are two really popular groups at my school – one of them is known as the really-nice-to-everyone group that doesn't make fun

> *I feel saddest when I'm left out or unwanted. I feel like this when people have huge parties and I'm not invited. LAUREN, 12*
>
> *I have a friend who will say something mean in front of people and because they are so scared to stick up for me, nobody does. ANNA, 9*
>
> *Most of the time people are popular not because of their personality, but because they wear the right clothes or their mother drives the right car. Normally the popular ones don't have a very nice personality at all. JENNIFER, 12*

of anyone in their group or in the other group. Then there's the 'I'm queen of all' and self-centered group. If you're not in their group you're open to humiliation," says Shelley.

"And my little circle of friends are friends with anyone. We're known as the group-who-will-accept-anyone. If they need someone to eat lunch with then they come to our table and that's fine. We accept them in. If someone is alone we say, 'You want to come sit with us?'"

So Shelley has decided she has certain principles she lives by –

NO MATTER WHAT.

They are the following:

1. She tries to be nice to everyone, whether they're popular or not.

2. She won't ditch her old friends to be with the popular group.

3. She doesn't place much stock in the idea of being popular, anyway.

There are other standards she tries to uphold, as well, but as far as popularity, this is as far as popularity goes.

In the end, the person whose approval you should seek is your own. Shelley has come to understand if she doesn't accept herself, who else would accept her? If she doesn't like herself, what person will? If she doesn't believe in herself, why would anyone else?

"Just be true to yourself – I can't stress it enough. I've had so many deadend friendships. I tried to change so much and when I finally got sick of changing for them, the friendship pretty much ended. They realized they could no longer change me. I only change now for a self improvement kind of thing – to make myself better, not to please someone else. I've worked really hard not to be jealous, not to talk about someone else. I still have weaknesses. Some people think only thin people or only pretty people are popular. Popularity is just how you see yourself."

I think someone is popular because they have friends and are kind. I don't think it should be who is pretty or is the best at something. Also being popular should not be a contest. I do consider myself popular because I have a lot of friends and I am kind to all of them. Also I include the people around me. ASHLEY, 13

I myself am sort of popular but I'm in the popular group and that sort of automatically makes you popular because you're accepted by them. STEPHANIE, 13

Being popular is all about having the most friends. I am the third least popular person in the class. I only have five friends!! SARAH, 12

I am quite popular. I have lots of friends. I'm friends with everyone in my class and a lot of people in my year. KERRI, 12

HOW IMPORTANT IS
POPULARITY TO YOU?

1. If a really popular girl told you that in order to be popular, you have to wear a certain style of clothes, you would . . .

  A. Ask your mother to take you shopping to buy a whole new wardrobe.

  B. Ask your friend to go with you to the mall and buy a couple trend-setting outfits.

  C. You'd tell her you're happy with your own personal style.

2. You know all the popular kids are going to meet outside the theater to go to the movies together. You decide to . . .

  A. Hang around the theater on the chance they might ask you to join them.

  B. Arrange to go with your friends to the same showing of the movie.

  C. Make your own plans with your friends to go to the mall for a special sale at your favorite store.

3. The MOST popular girl at your school makes fun of the outfit you're wearing.

  A. You fake that you're feeling sick so you can go home and change.

  B. You are completely crushed and have to fight back tears.

  C. You figure she's entitled to her opinion and you're entitled to yours.

4. The coolest kids at your school are going to someone's house to watch a movie your parents have forbidden you from seeing because they think it's unsuitable for you. You . . .

A. Lie to your parents saying that you'll be watching another movie they approve of.

B. Go to the house, hang around for awhile but when it's time to watch the movie, you make your excuse and leave.

C. You beg off this time but arrange to host another gathering at your house on another occasion.

5. There is a clique of really popular kids at your school, but they seem to be unkind and nasty to others outside their group.

A. You join them anyway.

B. You join them, but don't say anything too terribly mean.

C. You decide against joining them because they're too cruel, so you create your own group.

If you answered mostly As, you may have overrated popularity. You are trying too hard to be popular.

If you answered mostly Bs, you have a more realistic sense of the value of popularity.

If you answered mostly Cs, you understand that it's more important to be yourself than to compromise yourself to be popular!

7

Building a
Friendship

You know someone is your friend because they trust you, listen
to you, laugh with you and believe you. You know someone is
not your friend because they talk behind your back, ignore you
and laugh at you. LAURA, 13

I make new friends by having daily conversations with them and
being friendly. I keep them by being kind, including them in social
activities and always being talkative and cheerful. The qualitites I
think are most important in a friend are trust, secrecy, not being catty
or rude, respect, love, self-worth, kindness, funniness and more.
BROOKE, 12

Don't suck up to anyone! No friendships that begin with sucking up last. I just let people see my friendly side, and be nice. It's up to them from th
SHELLEY, 14

My secret to making new friends is being myself and being nice to them ar standing up for them. ROBIN, 11

I am usually the person that starts up the conversation. I ask the usual things: What's your name? How old are you? That kind of thing. JENNIFER, 12

I made new friends by talking and finding out about them. My secret to finding new friends is always to stay with them. Never neglect them. You know when someone is your friend because they like you and they hang around you. MANDEEP, 12

I think that it is very important to be able to talk with friends. When I talk with a friend, they seem very understandable. Maybe that's because they know what it is like. Some things my friends and I talk about are movies, boys, secrets, shopping, other friends, family and school. These are all the things my friends and I can talk about and know the other one is listening. ASHLEY, 13

I make friends by giving compliments and sometimes by just starting conversations. ANNA, 9

If I'm trying to make new friends at school, I go up to them and start talking. If we were on vacation and I knew where their apartment was, I would knock for them and see if they were coming out. After the vacation, I would keep in touch. KAYLEIGH, 13

girl to girl

LAUREN *Age 12*

Lives with: her mother, a nursing home administrator, and her dad, a teacher

Favorite food: pasta

Sports: skates in a precision ice skating team that competes nationally, loves playing catcher on her softball team, also plays field hockey after school

Other interests: music "I like Chicago, the Broadway musical. It's kind of weird but I like it. I really wanted to see the play because I love the music. My favorite song is "All That Jazz." I like to sing and dance to it – I'm a figure skater and I kind of like to make up skating programs to the music."

Friend philosophy: doesn't restrict herself to one particular clique of friends. "I consider myself a friendly person."

Girls understand the boundless value of friendship. They know how much fun it is to exchange notes in school with a pal. They love gabbing on the telephone, confiding their secret crushes to their best buds for hours at a time. They are totally psyched when they log onto their computer and hear "You've got mail!" – discovering their best mate has emailed them with a friendly "Waz up?" No matter how you look at it, life is better when you've got friends to share it with!

But, many girls wonder:
how do you make friends?

What might seem like the most natural thing in the world can be a mystery to many girls. They are totally mystified: Who should be my friend? How do your get her (or his) attention? Will they want to be my friend? How do you know when you can trust someone as a friend? What if I get hurt, disappointed, dumped or _____ (fill in the blank)?

Well, Lauren has been in that place. As an only child, she didn't have any brothers or sisters at home and so she has always felt friends have an especially important and significant place in her life. Lauren is close to her parents, but Lauren knows that there's a unique bond that can only be found in the companionship of friends. Her mother also recognizes the importance of friendship and has always encouraged Lauren to make friends. In fact, it was her mother who helped Lauren meet her first friend Katie when she was just a toddler.

It was convenient that Katie was the daughter of one of her

mother's closest friends. But the two little girls must have found they enjoyed each other's company for their own reasons because they're still friends – even to this day. They don't live in the same town, but they make it a point to spend time together, especially when their mothers visit one another.

"We just kind of got along. I'm still friends with her. I see her on the holidays at Christmas and stuff, or sometimes we get together for dinner and stuff," said Lauren.

Lauren decided early on that she had her own personal philosophy about friendship. She believed it was important to make as many friendships as possible. If one friend is fun, more are better! She realized there were lots of different people in the world she might enjoy getting to know and it seemed silly to her to limit herself. Her own individual style, then, was to be friendly and nice to everyone because you never know what might develop from there! Lauren is always ready with a friendly comment, a warm hello and an eager smile.

individual

I make friends by being nice and starting a good conversation to get to know them. I think that it is real important to be able to talk to your friends. I think that if you aren't able to talk to your friends, then I do not think that you are friends. I talk to my friends a lot. I talk to them as much as I can at school, at night or on the weekend. I call my friends. KELSEY, 12

I don't make new friends very easily. When I do make new friends, I try and treat them the same as all my other friends, otherwise they may feel left out. LAURA, 13

I usually wait a couple of days to get to know their personality and then if I like it, I'll ask if I can play with them and gradually get to know them. LAURA, 10

When I'm on holiday, if I see someone my own age, I just stare at them. When they look at me, I go over to them and talk to them. If I really like them, I give them my address and ask them to be my pen pal. SARAH, 12

When I'm making new friends I usually just try to be myself. It doesn't always work, but when it does, I'm happy to make a new friend. I can tell someone is my friend when they hang around me and save me seats and tell me things. MARGOT, 12

What Does it Take to Make a Friend?

RATE IN ORDER OF IMPORTANCE FROM 1 to 10 (1 which is most important to 10 which is least)

__ keep a friendly, open attitude

__ be willing to take a risk

__ be willing to make the first move

__ be persistent

__ know that you have something to offer as a friend

__ be patient

__ be interested

__ ask questions

__ don't be afraid to be hurt or disappointed

__ listen

Judge for yourself what you think it takes to make a new friend.

"My mom always said, 'You can never have enough friends.' I feel that she is right," said Lauren. "You try not to leave people out and stuff. You treat them nicely. They don't have to be your best friend but you treat them nicely because hopefully they will be the same to you."

But even with that positive social atttitude, Lauren found things

113

changing toward the end of fourth grade. Whereas all the girls seemed to get along before, she noticed that cliques were starting to form. It was really strange. Very weird. Not to mention a little bit competitive. All of a sudden, it didn't seem to matter that you were nice, what seemed to be important was if you **DRESSED NICE!!!** Definitely weird. Girls that had been popular and enjoyed many friendships weren't considered as cool if they didn't wear a certain style of clothes from a particular trendy (and expensive) store. The whole idea seemed really silly – even stupid – to Lauren!

You know you need to make a new friend . . .

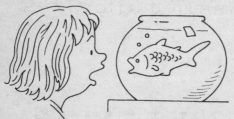

. . . when you find yourself confiding your innermost secrets and unfulfilled dreams to the goldfish.

. . . when you start considering the cast of the television show "Friends" your actual friends.

. . . when the idea of cleaning your room seems like a pleasant way to spend the day.

. . . when you consider your best friend is someone named FrouFrou, whom you have only met online and keep in touch with in a chat room.

. . . when the person closest to you is 3,000 miles away.

. . . when the word "zero" comes to mind when the word "friend" is said.

. . . when you have way too much time on your hands and way too few people to spend it with.

"I found it hard to fit in during elementary school. It was just like the beginning of fifth grade, at the end of the fourth, people started paying attention to what you wore. It was just that they kind of like judged you on what you wore instead what of you were like. I felt like a lot of this was ridiculous."

What should I do? Lauren wondered.

Should I try to change myself to be like the other girls in the clique? Should I beg my mother to buy me a new cool wardrobe? Should I just accept the fact that I'm a loser loner? None of those choices seemed to make sense to Lauren. Of course she wanted to be liked, she wanted to have friends, but she didn't want to pretend to be someone she wasn't.

"When I went into the middle school, I had a friend in one clique, a friend in another clique and a third friend in another clique. I didn't want to lose their friendship so I decided to be friendly to everyone," recalls Lauren.

Much of what Lauren describes is very normal. Girls are friends with one another for many reasons. Researchers have found that girls gain a sense of their own individuality through their connections with other girls. Seems strange doesn't it? That a girl would learn about herself only in relation to others. Experts have also found that when girls are young, a friend is someone to **play** with. But as they age, a friend is someone to **be** with. Girls look for both acceptance and identity from their friendships. Sometimes, the search for "who am I" can be found in the particular hairstyles we wear, certain expressions we use, or distinctive fashions we wear. Girls are often under pressure to act a certain way in

someone to be with

I make friends by talking to people and finding out all about them. We exchange secrets and learn to trust each other. I treat them with respect and value their need for space and privacy. It is very important to be able to talk to your friends and trust your friends. We talk about problems we may be having, our families, other friends that maybe we might have had an argument with or something. We do share secrets with each other. We tell each other about fears or worries we have which we do not want anyone else to know about. RACHEL, 12

I've found that it helps to listen to problems your friends may be having and not to just brush them aside. Be understanding and give advice. STEPHANIE, 13

I find new friends by sitting near them and asking them lots of questions and talking together. CAROLYNE, 12

First I ask her what her/his name is and then we just start chatting. EMMA, 12

I make new friends by telling jokes and being crazy. BRITTANY, 12

I introduce myself to new people in the school or just people I haven't met. SARAH, 12

I feel that I'm nice to lots of people and making friends just starts with a "hello." There is no big secret. Finding good friends can be hard but once you've found one nice person who is a good friend to you, do stuff together, talk to them and hang around with them. LAUREN, 12

order to be seen a certain way – and this is even more true as they grow up into a more complex social scene. But not all girls cave into the pressure.

Fortunately for Lauren, one particular friendship helped her enormously. When Lauren had moved on to the middle school, she met Natasha. They were in all the same classes together and very often were assigned seats next to each other too!

"We just kind of shared the same interests. "We'd just talk to

new level of closeness

each other in every class. We're
both softball players, we really like it,
and we like the same kind of music. She would
always invite me downtown to go with her and all of her
friends. She would invited me to the movies a couple of times
with her other friends too," says Lauren.

"Natasha was really nice. She liked me and she was one of those
girls who wore the right clothes. She introduced me to the other
people in the group, and so I became friends with everyone. And I
didn't change myself but it took awhile to fit in."

Then one day Lauren asked her mother if it would be okay if
Lauren slept over. Lauren sensed that she and Natasha were getting
closer and it seemed like a good time to bring their friendship to a
new level of closeness. Lauren casually mentioned the sleepover to
Natasha at school and a couple of weeks later, the overnight visit
was arranged. The girls watched a rented movie on the VCR,
snacked on popcorn and then talked for a long while, each
stretched out in sleeping bags on couches in the family room. They
talked so long, Lauren doesn't quite remember when they each fell
off to sleep.

"We were up for awhile. I thought we were really getting
closer," says Lauren. Their friendship has continued to grow, and
Lauren's friendships with others have also continued to grow.
Through Natasha, she's met a lot of the other kids in her group,
but she's also met kids who belong to other cliques, too. And
Lauren has kept to her basic friend philosophy: make as many
friends as possible – regardless of cliques!

"Before school, there's like this 15 minute period and we like

117

hangout all together. Then in classes, Natasha is in all my classes and some of the people from the other cliques are in some of my classes so we all sit together. When I entered the middle school there were a ton of cliques but I don't hang out with one group. There are a bunch of cliques and I'm not with one specific clique – I'm friends with people in all of them."

LAUREN'S TIPS FOR MAKING NEW FRIENDS:

- Try not to leave people out
- Treat everyone nicely
- Always be open to new friendships
- Be *friendly* – that's the best way to be friends
- Don't limit yourself to one group of friends
- Be true to yourself, then you will find your true friends

But even if you're friendly to everyone, can everyone be your friend? Not really, says Lauren. Nor would you want everyone to be your friend. Some people, after all, may not be the best choice in the friend department. And that's some of what girls must decided for themselves. Who is a suitable friend? Who is trustworthy? Who is going to really be there for you? Lauren believes that's the toughest part of starting a friendship – figuring out who you **WANT** to be your friends.

"It's hard because you have to know who the right kids are," explains Lauren. "You don't want to pick people doing drugs because that's not right. You want to make sure you feel comfortable that if you tell them something that you don't want them to tell, that the person is somebody who is trustworthy. You want to make sure they treat others with respect and they're not making fun of someone all the time. Otherwise, what would stop them from making fun of me?"

According to researchers, girls are not just looking for a friend with a smiling face. They want a friend who has character. They want someone with whom they can connect, grow close and share intimacies! They want someone who will get their jokes, will listen to them sympathetically, will share themselves. Perhaps someone they admire, think brave, and laugh with. Whatever the characteristics girls seek out in a friend, they know what they are looking for.

119

"I just want someone I can count on to be there when I need them – even when I don't need them. Someone to talk to and stuff, to tell them things and to just be yourself around them."

Lauren feels happy and pleased her plan has worked. She now counts many kids as her friends. She rarely feels lonely or bored. She can always think of someone to call to invite somewhere or confide something. Whether she's at school, or at home on the weekends, she feels fortunate to have the company of friends almost anytime she wants it.

Lauren also feels good about herself when she feels she can make – and keep – friends. Researchers believe our ability to create satisfying relationships with others gives us a sense of self-esteem

I'm a really shy person so I find it hard to make new friends. Most of the time they come up to me so I don't have to do anything. But if they don't then we don't talk. KERRI, 12

I make new friends by going and talking to people. I easily keep my friends by being nice and being myself. It is really important to be able to talk to friends. That is one way you know you can trust your friend and see if they are true friends or not. CODIE, 12

I love making new friends. The way I like to be friendly is, for example, when I play netball, I always say hello to the opponent I'm standing next to. If they start talking to me, I'll talk back. Of course, this doesn't always work, but it works most of the time! HANNAH, 12

and a sense of our own value.

"It makes me feel wanted to be with good friends. I hate it when I feel left out and stuff. It makes me feel good to know someone likes me as a friend. It makes me feel happy. It's good to have a variety of friends because it gets me out of the whole clique situation."

Then Lauren adds,

> **"You just want to be nice to them – you want to treat them the way you want to be treated."**

HOW FRIENDLY

1. You are going to a new school for the first time. You . . .

A. Hang back, be quiet, and watch. You're afraid to mix.

B. You smile a lot, say hi to people you don't know and act friendly.

C. You decide you will never find a friend. You wish you were back at your old school.

2. You notice a girl who seems very nice and are interested in getting to know her.

A. You wait and hope she'll make the first move.

B. The next time you see her, you say hi and introduce yourself.

C. You're convinced there's no way she'd ever notice you. You give up.

3. You have been assigned to work on a project with the most popular girl in the school.

A. You are so nervous, you can barely speak to her about the assignment.

ARE YOU?

B. You are eager for the chance to get to know her.

C. You are sure this girl would rather work with someone else, so you ask the teacher if you can work on the project by yourself instead.

4. **You've made the soccer team, but you don't know a single other teammate.**

A. You wonder if this was a good idea to go out for the team after all.

B. You look forward to your first practice and hope you will be making lots of new friends.

C. You decide to quit the team rather than risk being embarrassed in front of strangers.

If you answered mostly As, you are beginning to learn how to live with risk. Whenever you face a new social situation and the possibilities of meeting new friends, it's a risk. But it's often a risk worth taking.

If you answered mostly Bs, then you have the kind of open and friendly attitude that will win you friends wherever you go. You obviously have a healthy confidence in yourself – and in your ability to make friends. Terrific!

If you answered mostly Cs, you seem afraid to take risks. Perhaps you've been hurt in friendships before so, understandably, you feel cautious, but you may need to learn to trust again.

My Best Friend Won't Talk to Me –

Now What Do I Do?

Normally the thing we fall-out about is friendship, like I want to be best friends with one girl but another girl is her best friend and she'll hate me and so will another best friend. So, see how confusing and irritating this is? HANNAH, 12

One of my friends called me on the phone and said I was being mean to her. She was making me feel very bad and after she had hung up, I started crying. I was very sad and miserable for awhile and I did not want to call her back. Eventually, she called me back and said her sorrys and how she had been crying and I said my sorrys and how I'd been crying. We don't get in really big fights anymore and I'm glad about that. MARGOT, 12

I got into a big fight with one of my best friends for trying to stick up for myself. After two weeks of not talking to each other, I called her on the phone and we made up. ANNA, 9

There was one time when my best friend and I broke up. She didn't like me because this other girl said I said something behind her back (which I didn't). But we made up. I just kept telling her I didn't do it. Then one day she asked me if I wanted to make up. She believed me. KAYLEIGH, 13

I usually fight with my friends if they break a promise or tell a secret or do something to hurt another one of my friends. I usually solve my disagreements with friends by telling them what I think and then let them explain why they did whatever they did. LAURA, 10

Just the other day I had an argument with a friend and the second I realized that there was a friendship in danger, it was like alarm bells went off. So as fast as I could I sorted it all out and accepted that I was wrong and I think people really treasure it if you can admit your mistakes and be willing to take responsibility for your actions. STEPHANIE, 13

When my friends and I fight, we fight about things like who said this, who said that, things about lying, keeping secrets and things like that. They are always little things like that. The way I handle them is by talking to the person and seeing why they did something. ASHLEY, 13

We normally fall out if one of us feels left out. That's how I broke up with my two friends. I handle the disagreement by falling out and leaving them alone. After that they often phone me to apologize. SARAH, 12

I haven't had much luck with friends. One of my best friends in my primary school always hit and punched me for no reason. She also got me into lots of trouble. In the end, I'd had enough and I told her. I haven't heard from her since. She even forgot my birthday which I never forgave her for. KERRI, 12

BROOKE Age 12

Lives with: her mom, a substitute school nurse, her dad, an airline pilot, her two brothers, ages 15 and 11

Favorite food: chicken pot pie and mashed potatoes

Pets: none, her dad is allergic to fur

Pet Peeve: when her brothers touch her stuff, especially when they use her toiletries like her body wash

Hobbies: plays soccer, after school sports, takes art classes, performs in community theater productions and enjoys reading. "I'm very picky about books. I like reading books about girls' lives. I don't like books that are fantasies."

Future career: not sure. "I know I don't want to be a teacher. I love art and stuff like that. I also like talking to people about their problems."

Any girl will tell you, the best, most brilliant days ever are those when she is hanging out with her best friend doing something they really enjoy together. Maybe it's having private time together talking about the new boy in their class. Perhaps it's walking to school giggling and being incredibly silly. Or it might be riding bikes, side by side, on a sunny day, down to the park. Most girls will also say that their worst days imaginable are when they have a fight with their best friend. Sometimes it might be a huge disagreement over some stupid piddling thing. Or perhaps it's a little misunderstanding

over her not waiting for you after school. Maybe, it's a case of outright betrayal. Whatever the circumstances, when friends aren't talking, they aren't connected and that is always a painful, upsetting and unsettling experience for everyone involved.

What to do?

Nearly every girl – at some time in her life – has been in that awful place of being alone and upset and confused because a friend is mad at her. Chances are you have too. Maybe you've had an argument and you know exactly what the issue is all about or perhaps you don't understand at all what's going on and feel totally clueless! Brooke has been there, too. Most days, when Brooke wakes up, she's in a good mood and looking forward to her day, but there was a time last summer when she thought her whole world had unraveled like a badly-knit sweater. It was a time when something terrible occured between her and her best friend Kate. Brooke had never had anything this big or this bad happen between her and a friend. For the most part she and her friends generally all get along together. And that was what was so weird about what happened. It caught her completely off-guard.

Actually, the whole summer had been pretty fun. She'd spent tons of time with Kate. Nearly everyday Kate would call or she would call Kate and the two would make plans. Some days they would go to the pool. Sometimes they would walk downtown and go shopping. Other days they would just hang out at Brooke's or Kate's house. Whatever they decided to do on any particular day always was great because whenever they were together, they were having fun.

"We played like everyday, all summer. We were the best of friends. We went to the pool, hung out, got lunch, played in the neighborhood," says Brooke. "We were friends – nothing was wrong. Everything was fine. We were just like hanging out and talking and stuff like we always have. We've been friends since fifth grade, hanging out, helping each other."

Then, another girl that Kate was also best friends with came home from summer camp where she'd been away all summer. Brooke didn't think much about it at the time. She didn't consider it a big deal, because she felt sure that she and Kate had a tight, unbreakable bond, that nothing – or no one – could come between them. But Brooke couldn't have been more wrong.

I have been through the ringer with friends. It seems every year, I have another broken friendship to count, but I don't mind. Looking back, I see how hurtful they were (making threats, full of themselves, rude and selfish). One is still in my circle of friends. I try to be as polite as possible, but I wouldn't trust her again. SHELLEY, 14

One time I had a problem with my best friend because we both liked the same boy. We had problems but now we don't because she likes another boy and he lives far, far away. ROBIN, 11

TOP 10 WAYS TO RECOGNIZE A PAL PROBLEM

1. Your friend doesn't return your phone calls.

2. All of a sudden, your friend has gotten "busy."

3. People come up to you asking, "Are you mad at _____ (fill in the name of your friend)?

4. She ignores you.

5. She doesn't talk to you.

6. She makes plans with other people without letting you know or including you.

7. She is mean to you.

8. She talks about you to other people.

9. She doesn't sit with you.

10. She gives you evil looks.

At the end of the summer, just before school began, a lot of the kids Brooke is friends with had made a plan to go to the movies. Kate was going too. When Brooke got home she asked her mother if she could go, and after getting permission, she called Kate about carpooling to the movies.

"She said, 'I'm kind of carpooling with someone else. We're going to go downtown and get some supper.' When I told my mom, she said, 'Don't go, Brooke. Someone is only going to get their feelings hurt. Kate would have invited you if she wanted you to come.' But I didn't listen. I asked Kate, 'Can you save me a seat?' She said, 'Sure.' But she was kind of uneasy about it so she was kind of blowing me off. But I went anyway. I just wanted to be in the loop. I wanted to be with my friends. It's kind of a cool thing to do to go to the movies, so I just dismissed the thought and went."

"I got dropped off and I didn't see really anyone because I was kind of late. I got my ticket and went in and saw a big group – it was like 20 kids. I said, 'Oh Kate. Hi. You didn't save me a seat." And she said, 'I was the last one in the row and I couldn't.' I said, 'Okay.'

There was a free row in front of the group, so Kate sat in an empty row all by herself. It felt awkward and goofy and she really wanted company. She looked like a total loser all by herself. She turned back to Kate and the others and begged, "Come on, guys, can you come up and sit with me? I don't want to sit alone." But, as Brooke remembers, they were talking to the boys behind them. Brooke persisted.

"I was trying to get their attention. I was trying to talk to them. I said, 'Please you guys? Please?'" says Brooke. For a few minutes

You know someone is not your friend when they talk bad about you, they annoy you, they leave you out, they lie. SHELLEY 14

When I was about seven or eight I was "best friends" with three girls. The four of us were always going everywhere together. Suddenly, one day one of them refused to let me speak to or play with her or any of the others. I felt so sad and lonely and like no one cared about me. I felt that there was no one to talk to and that there was something wrong with me because everyone else had a friend and I didn't. JENNIFER, 12

We fight when someone is rude to the other person or when one person isn't invited to a party. We just say sorry to handle it. BRITTANY, 12

I have been hurt by a friend. She hit me in the face because I did not hang around with her at break. EMMA, 12

I feel the saddest when my friend goes off with someone else and tells her about her problems and doesn't come and tell her close friends. My friend did this to me and I was very upset. MANDEEP, 12

she sat in another empty chair closer to the group, but it was next to two boys who are always causing trouble. She didn't want to stay there either.

"I went out of the theater and I was going to call my mother because there was no point in staying. But then some other friends came in the theater and said, 'Oh come and sit with us.' I watched a movie – that was fine. After the movie, they all came out and I was waiting for my dad and they all walked across the street. No one came up to me, no one even asked me if I wanted to go with them. They didn't even turn back. They recognized me standing there – they just didn't even think about me."

> It was one of the most painful, humiliating, horrid moments of her life. **Ever.**

She felt completely alone and abandoned. She was shattered. Why had Kate ignored her? What kind of friend would betray another like that? How could Kate be so cruel?

Many girls have felt exactly the same torturous emotions as Brooke, wondering: How can friends treat each other so horribly? What evil possesses them to ditch someone so close to them? What can you do to protect yourself from such pain? And how do you deal with it once it happens?

"I got home and told my mom what happened. She said, 'I told you Brooke.' I was crying. She was telling me what she told me before – that once Kate's other friend had come back from camp, Kate had stopped calling me," says Brooke. "She totally ditched me. Every time I would call her, she'd say, 'I can't play today. I can't play today.'"

"I told my mom, 'I'm not talking to her. She's an idiot.' Mom said, 'You don't do that, Brooke. She's still your friend. You can't treat her like that. If you see her in the hall, you be friendly. When she calls you the next time, you can just say no. But if you really want to know if she's still your friend, you need to confront her. Talk to her – maybe you're taking this the wrong way. I said, 'No mom, I can't do that. I can't confront her. It's too hard. She'll probably go back to her friend and say Brooke is such a wimp, she felt terrible after the movies.'"

Brooke felt **SO** confused and conflicted. Should she risk saying anything to Kate? Should she just try and forget about it? Forget about Kate? Forget about their friendship? She felt angry and hurt. She wanted to scream at Kate and tell her off, but she knew she could never really do that. But, then, again, what exactly should she do?

"Finally I got the guts to talk to her. I said, **'You really hurt my feelings. Why did you do that?'** She knew what she did and she knew what she did was wrong because as soon as I said it, she said that when they had walked across the street she had asked, 'Where's Brooke?' and someone else said, 'Her dad picked her up.' I don't think that was the truth. But at least I told her how I felt and that it really made me sad."

Brooke says she is glad that she mustered the courage to confront Kate, although she said it has not made everything go back to the way it was. She and Kate are back to being chummy, but Brooke doesn't yet feel **100 percent confidence** in Kate's friendship. She's not entirely comfortable and can't yet depend on her completely again.

WAYS TO SAVE A FRIENDSHIP

1. **THINK.** Try to figure out the cause of the problem between the two of you.

2. **TALK.** Confront your friend and explain your feelings and your concern.

3. **LISTEN.** Hear her side of the situation.

4. **ACT.** Work on changing your behavior, or on accepting hers.

"I don't trust her as much. She's a nice kid and I like her a lot. I like her personality and I like to be around her, but if she's going to do that to me, I don't know what else she'd do to me so I hold back some," explains Brooke.

Brooke does feel very proud of the way she handled the situation, even though she doesn't like confrontations – just as most girls don't. Many girls have difficulty expressing their anger because they fear it's not nice. They worry if they tell someone they've been hurt, they're hurting someone else. They're concerned they will have broken the cardinal rule of girlhood: girls are supposed to be nice! Brooke speaks for many girls when she says, "I hate doing that. I hate confronting someone. I don't want anyone to feel bad. I want everyone to be happy, but I just had never experienced anything like that. That was just pure meanness. That was way too catty for me."

Brooke has learned something from this rather painful episode of personal history. She's learned that while she doesn't want to

> Once I got in a fight with my best friend's sister and she got mad at me. I was really sad, but we made up the next day. CODIE, 12

> I feel really sad when I break up with people, especially my best friend but I can't break up with anybody for long because I make them laugh and they tell me their problems or whatever is wrong and we're back to being best buddies again! HANNAH, 12

> When I first met her she lied about all sorts of things like she said she came from Hawaii, had a twin brother and sister when she really has a brother that is 7 and a sister 10 and she was born right here. But all of that was a year ago and we sorted it out by her telling the truth and we forgot about it. Sort of. JENNIFER, 12

> I felt very sad when my friend and I had a big argument and called each other some horrible names. I felt very guilty afterwards. That made me feel horrible. We didn't speak for weeks. I talked to my other friends about it and they gave me some advice. RACHEL, 12

> I had one problem with not a very close friend. It started with a small situation and that led to a big situation. We sorted this out by talking it over. MANDEEP, 12

hurt anyone's feelings, she also can't hurt herself by hiding her own feelings. It's important to speak up when a friend has hurt you. Maybe it was an intentional slight, or perhaps not. If you don't ask, they might not tell. A friendship should offer lots of warm and cozy feelings, but it also needs to be able to accommodate conflict, too. It's a girl's nature to want everyone to be happy all the time, but that's perhaps unrealistic. Two people are not always going to agree on everything, see things the same exact way, or share the same perspective. But a true friendship will bend, adapt to, and hopefully resolve, conflicts.

Honesty is very important because if they lie about something then how can you trust them again. Trustworthiness is also very important, you've got to be able to trust them otherwise you haven't got much of a friendship. If you haven't got a sense of humor, then you take everything the wrong way and you get stressed with everyone. KERRI, 12

We fight about silly things sometimes like why one person got a higher test result when we both did the same amount of studying. Or who is the cleverest out of all of us. I would usually keep my distance for a little while, then I would go and apologize. RACHEL, 12

We fight about feeling left out. And lonely. We handle disagreements by telling each other and we try to include them. SARAH, 12

When I have been hurt by a friend, we talk about it and decide whether we will still be friends or if we feel we need a break from each other. Whatever we decide we carry out and then we always end up being friends again, eventually. LAURA, 13

I'm the saddest when I'm in a fight with a friend, or feel left out. I used to be very jealous when I was left out by a friend, but I've been trying hard not to anymore. My friends have been in many fights with each other. (I'm usually kind of in between.) But, we always seem to come out alive. Like my buddy Laurie says, "What doesn't kill us, makes us stronger." SHELLEY, 14

When we fight we either talk to one of our other friends about it, sort it out by talking to each other or we give each other time to cool off! JENNIFER, 12

"If someone is going to hang out with me and they totally blow me off, it tells me something about them. Maybe I should leave them awhile and come back when they'll actually treat me nicely. I'm not going to stay mad at that person if I've had a friendship a long time or just forget about it, either. I am going to talk to someone because I really care, I will confront them," says Brooke.

Brooke explains that sometimes there are small misunderstandings between friends, what she calls "silent fights" over finding out, for example, that somebody said something about you, or told a secret they promised they wouldn't, or gave you the cold shoulder.

Most of the time we fight over stupid little things like someone not waiting for them at breaktime to go to the cantine. We stop talking for about two hours then we just start talking again. KERRI, 12

Once there was a time where I was hurt by a joke that my friend made. She said that I was stupid and I didn't know that it was a joke. I said to her, "Why did you call me stupid?" And she was sorry, she thought I knew it was a joke. LAURA, 10

It is so important to be able to talk to my three best friends. We talk about everything – boys, other friends, each other and our families. Some very important secrets are told between friends and when you're in the dark, I find it easier to talk and to tell secrets. These things are vital in friends: trustworthiness, having a sense of humor, looking pretty, kindness, listening to all your problems, never telling your secrets – even if you do fall out. HANNAH, 12

We rarely fight with each other. If we do fight, it's about boys but we talk about it and sort it out. RAWINDER, 13

My friends and I fight about anything you can think of, from stupid little things to pretty big things. To handle a disagreement, we usually have our space and forget about it. MARGOT, 12

I really have never gotten into a fight with one of my friends. When Gretchen and I were little we would have little friend fights and get over the fight in about a minute. KELSEY, 12

"I'm a really sensitive person. I always come home from school saying things like, 'She was giving me the cold shoulder.' My mother says, 'Brooke don't take it to heart. You always take things too seriously. They probably didn't even see you and you just go on and on about it.' I eventually say to them, 'Hi do you want to come over?' And I realized maybe they were just in a bad mood that day."

Making and keeping and caring for friends is a very complicated

True or False

1. If you and your friend disagree, you should talk about it. ___ T ___ F

2. If your feelings have been hurt by a friend, you should always swallow your pain. ___ T ___ F

3. When you sense your friend is being dishonest with you, you should confront her. ___ T ___ F

4. I can't imagine staying mad at my friends for long. ___ T ___ F

5. I will do anything to avoid fighting with my friends. even if it means giving up something really important.. ___ T ___ F

6. Once a friend disappoints or hurts me. that's it. I am never their friend again. ___ T ___ F

business, which is weird and wacky because it should be one of the most natural things in the world, shouldn't it? But, the truth is, friendships are works in progress. They take time, energy, caring and thought. And sometimes things don't always go the way we would like, because, everyone is different and no one agrees with each other all the time.

No friendship is perfect because as Brooke realizes, "I really don't think anyone's perfect."

Friends?

1. True. It's important in a friendship to be able to discuss differences.

2. False. People who swallow their pain can make themselves sick. Squelching feelings can lower your immune system and cause other health issues. It's important to keep your relationships honest by being honest!

3. True. It's okay to overlook mistakes, but if you suspect your friend is not treating you honestly and with respect, then it's important to address this, or else your friendship is based on falsehoods and lies.

4.True. It's okay to feel anger, but fuming and festering is not healthy. It's important to address conflicts and then **GET OVER IT!**

5. False. It's impossible to avoid conflicts. It's better to accept that conflict is a healthy part of being in a relationship and learn how to resolve them. It means people are really relating!

6. False. Being a friend means also being able to forgive and forget.

9

What's the Big Deal About Having Friendships?

I'm an only child so sometimes I get lonely or bored. All my friends are like my brothers or sisters because we have good moments and bad ones. My friends and I are there for each other. LAUREN, 12

The best thing about friendship is that they're always there whenever you need them. MANDEEP, 12

You need to talk to your friends. It can get you down if you don't tell someone what's wrong. You can talk to them about growing up, boys, family and things like that. I felt my friends totally understood me when my grandad died. They all helped me through it. KAYLEIGH, 13

The two most important factors of friendship are honesty and trustworthiness. Without these what have you got in a friendship? STEPHANIE, 13

I think that you need to be able to trust your friend, be able to rely on them to keep a secret and be honest so you don't hurt your friend. I think the most important thing is to be able to trust your friends because trust is the base of friendship and without trust you don't have friendship. LAURA, 10

I know that someone is my friend because they talk to me, we get along together, I like him or her, and we play together. I think the best thing about friendship is that you can trust your friends and I think that is very important because you can tell someone what is going on and you can trust them that they won't tell anyone. KELSEY, 12

It is easier to talk to my friends than it is to talk to my mother. I talk to my friends about worries, problems, questions and gossip. I think honesty, dependability and trustworthiness are the most important qualities in a friendship. LAURA, 13

ANNA *Age 12*

Lives with: her mother, a nurse, and her dad, who works in a library

Best-in-school-friend: Cheryl "We agree on nearly everything, except our handwriting!!"

Best-out-of-school-friend: Natalie "It kind of started in playgroup – we must have been about 3 or 4. I just met her and from there, we were just friends. We've been friends for a very long time and we are still friends in high school."

Favorite hobbies: enjoys swimming, shopping and going to theme parks

Pets: a two-year-old hamster named Eddie. "He's completely bald. He's got these mites and he got an injection but it didn't work so he's completely bald, but he's very lively."

Anna's name is a palindrome which means her name is spelled the same both forward and backward. Anna's really aware of patterns like that. She's aware, for instance, that every fall she looks forward to going to school and at the start of every summer, she is sad to be separated from her friends.

"At the beginning of the new term or year is when I am most happy because I get to be with my friends and my best friend Cheryl. That means that we also have to catch up on gossip," says Anna.

"I feel the saddest at the end of the term and school year. It means that I don't see my friends as much as when I'm at school."

Anna is very attached to her friends. She's not at all unlike most girls whose friendships are central to the whirl and motion of their lives. Girls enjoy each other's company. They love to talk, gossip, talk, shop, talk, play sports, talk, go to movies, talk, have

The best thing about friendship is that you can always rely on your friends to be there for you. You will always have someone to talk to and to share your secrets with. Without my friends I would lead a boring and lifeless life. Kerri, 12

You know someone is your friend by just a feeling in your heart. Codie, 12

A friend is someone who you can talk to, usually about anything. I think that is the best thing. Rachel, 12

It is very important you can share embarrassing moments. We come up with everything to talk about. From clouds, to dreams to boys. You know someone is your friend when they don't tease you and you feel you can share your secrets. Sarah, 12

Friends are people who care about you and who really know you. If something is wrong with you, they'll know it. Brittany, 12

kinetic energy

sleepovers and talk! They never tire of talk. The world is an exciting, interesting, changing place and girls like to share their impressions of it by talking about it. It's their way of understanding themselves and their place in the world. It's like this strange kinetic energy: you put two girls in the same room and they'll just gravitate towards each other!

That weird kinetic energy has drawn Anna to her oldest friend Natalie. She can't really explain why their friendship began because it's so old a relationship she was too young to remember it actually beginning! She knows she and Natalie were in playgroup together. They were only 3 or 4 at the time. For some reason, they were attracted to each other like magnets and the next thing you know, they were friends. Amazing.

Well, it wasn't quite that straightforward, actually, because there was this complicating factor. Natalie already had two best friends, a set of twins with whom she was really very close and there wasn't much other room for Anna too. Anna vaguely remembers Natalie's sixth birthday party and she had a blow-up bouncy castle and the twins were there. She wasn't too jealous of their friendship because she knew Natalie liked her. And then, the twins moved away about seven years ago so there was suddenly room for a bigger friendship with Anna.

"We'd been playing together and I was kind of like one of her closest friends, but after the twins moved she had no one to play with and we just hung out together and we thought we'd be best friends. She just wanted to be best friends. She didn't really say anything, she just started inviting me round for tea. This would be after school and on the weekends," recalls Anna.

"She was **really, really funny** – she still is. She's got a really good sense of humor, she just makes me laugh. She used to talk in a funny accent that used to set me off because I'm quite a giggly person and that's why. She's got a really good sense of humor – **really, really good**."

For Anna, sharing a good laugh is a cornerstone of a key friendship. Anna admires how Natalie is not afraid to act the class clown – she's so good at it! "Ooooh, she so silly!" says Anna. Sometimes, we choose our friends because of the qualities we admire in them. Sometimes those qualities are personality traits we wish we had ourselves. For Anna, she appreciates Natalie's bold and brash side in school, the way she sometimes – quite literally – will stand out because she's standing up in class making jokes. Of course, her sense of humor is not the only thing she enjoys about Natalie. She know's Natalie's quieter side, as well.

"We go swimming together and mess around. We go shopping in the town. We usually buy the same things. A couple of weeks ago I bought a top and she bought the same one – it was yellow. I like stationery. I bought this really nice pen and she did too," says Anna.

When Anna and Natalie buy the same clothes or pens, it's a **visible way of affirming their friendship**. They can not only write notes to each other to keep their connection going, they can write it using the same exact pen! How much more together can you get than that? Girls are always searching for ways to swear their allegiance to each other, to declare their unbreakable bonds to one another, and assert their unwavering friendship. How else do you explain the popularity of "friendship" necklaces or rings in which each half of a heart is worn by one friend? Our friendships are so unbelievably significant, we want the whole world to know about them. Imagine. Kind of strange and wonderful, isn't it?

And in a way, by declaring our friendships publicly by wearing the same clothes or buying the same CDs, we are, in effect, saying, "This is who I am. This is who we are."

"I think we usually like the same things," says Anna of Natalie. "We don't really disagree on hardly anything. We hardly fall out. We like the same teachers. We've got a very nice teacher and we both like him. We both like swimming, we like film, and we both kind of like school."

How do girls find out all this about each other? Well, they talk, of course. Communicating is that powerful glue that sticks us to each other, that keeps us connected.

"I think somebody's your friend when you hang around together, you talk to them and you do things together," says Anna.

Like most girls, Anna has found that sharing the good times and the bad **with a friend** makes everything better. Friends can give us a high five when we've aced that wretched test we were so worried about and friends can hold our hand when we are frightened or sad or lonely or worried.

"One of my close friends has got serious family problems which I can't tell, sorry, but sometimes it helps her to talk about it. We also talk about which boys we fancy and girl problems such as puberty. I think that the most important things in a friendship is **trustworthiness and dependability**. If they asked you to keep a secret you wouldn't tell anybody," says Anna. "The best thing about friendship is that you always have someone to talk to. And when you're stuck or you've got a problem, you know you've got a friend to talk to and support."

Of course, even among the best

I think it's very important to be able to talk with your friends. If you can't talk, you know you can't really trust them. My friends and I talk about friends (fights, etc.), teachers, boys (I usually listen and give advice since I don't "like" anyone), parents, things we did with other friends, qualities we like in others, and things we are going to do. I tell my best friends about what's bugging me, who I like (when I do like someone), and things I'm thinking about in life. **SHELLEY, 14**

We like to go shopping, swimming, to the movies, have sleepovers and we go to the theater. We talk about any problems we may be having, friends, family, we make up stories, what we are doing Saturday, that sort of thing. I think it is important that you can trust all of your friends completely. I think that honesty is important and so is a sense of humor. I tell my friends everything, like that my nan has Alzheimer's or if I have a problem. I tell my friends more than I tell my mum. **JENNIFER, 12**

She totally understood. **SARAH, 12**

147

> *I was at camp and it was after taps but my friend and I were talking. I could tell her whatever I wanted and she understood. I understood what she was saying also. We talked about our family and things that have been going on or things that we thought about family situations we have been in.*
> **ASHLEY, 13**

> *My friend always makes me feel accepted. Around her I don't put on a show. I just act myself.* **LAUREN, 12**

"best friends" or in any developing relationship, there is bound to be some conflict, sometime. As close as two people can become, it's perfectly normal to have moments when they don't agree or when there is a clash or some other conflict. It could be about anything. It could be a huge, bad-tempered argument or it might be a cold-shouldered standoff. Whatever the problem, though, a strong friendship will be able to accommodate differences and resolve them. Working through a conflict can be the toughest challenge there is to a friendship. Feelings get hurt, friends feel angry and the fallout is horrible. **It can be incredibly painful, lonely and agonizing to be out of sync with someone who means so much!!**

FRIENDSHIP IS A TWO-WAY STREET

It takes two people to make a friendship. You know you've picked the right pal when . . .

. . . You're the first person she wants to talk to about a problem.

. . . She's the first person you go to to talk about your problem.

. . . You wouldn't hesitate to borrow clothes from her.

. . . You wouldn't hesitate to let her borrow your clothes.

. . . You never run out of things to talk about.

. . . You could trust her with any secret.

. . . She could trust you with any of her secrets.

. . . You know her favorite color, singer and school subject.

. . . She knows the same about you.

. . . She laughs at all your jokes.

. . . You think she's wickedly funny.

. . . You stick up for her.

. . . She sticks up for you.

. . . You never find each other boring.

. . . Life is better when you're together!

"We've had really nasty fights and our parents had to help us kind of get back together but we haven't had any in a while. Once I liked this girl and Natalie didn't like her. I started to spend more time with her and Natalie got a bit jealous. We had a really big argument. We couldn't agree. We didn't talk to each other for a couple of days and then we just got a bit lonely without each other. Life wasn't the same. I made the first move. I was saying we can't keep going like this. We just started talking and we agreed I couldn't see the other girl more because Natalie wasn't comfortable with it. I did like the other girl, but, in the end, she got another friend and I kept hanging around with Natalie," says Anna.

It's not the only time Anna has had to figure out how to juggle more than one friendship at a time. Anna met her friend Cheryl last year in school. "I got chatty to Cheryl and we started hanging around together and only a couple of months ago we became best friends because she broke up with her other best friend," recalls Anna. "Natalie knows about Cheryl. Natalie is quite comfortable with me being best friends with two people. She's quite comfortable . . . yeah."

Anna's been able to make this arrangement work because she has been mindful to make each friend feel important to her. She tries hard to include each of them equally in her life. The three often go shopping together, for instance. And whenever there is a potential problem, they either take some time to think things over or talk it out.

"I think girls are better at sorting themselves out," says Anna.

Negotiating a friendship can sometimes require the skills of a diplomat. And it seems that girlhood is the training camp for learning all sorts of codes of friendship. How do you maintain multiple friendships without hurting anyone? When is it okay to talk about one friend with another? How close a friendship do I need and want? What is trust? Who do I feel comfortable sharing my secrets with? There are a gazillion questions girls have about friendship from how to make friends to how to keep them. And whatever girls learn about their relationships, they will rely on the rest of their lives.

Developing strong relationships, understanding and accepting differences between people, and being dependable are just a few of the skills girls will need while sitting with a friend in the classroom today and in the boardroom they might be in tomorrow! The skills of friendship they are grooming today will prepare them to be happier, more successful grownups later on. We are learning who we are and we want our friends to validate that so that we might continue to grow.

"All the friends I've ever had accepted me the way I was deep down," says Anna.

THE BEST THINGS ABOUT FRIENDSHIP . . .

The best thing about a friend is being able to talk to them. When you can really talk to a friend and tell them how you feel, it makes you feel good to have friends.
ASHLEY, 13

The best thing about friendship is the company. I would be unhappy without friends to have fun with.
SARAH, 12

The best thing about friendship is laughing, joking around and having a good time. Friendship would be very boring if there was no fun, so definitely, the best thing is fun, fun, FUN! STEPHANIE, 13

The best thing about friendship is that you always have somebody to talk to and someone you can really confide in. I would always try and be friends with somebody because I hate being on my own and being a loner – I love chatting! HANNAH, 12

The best thing about friendship is you have someone to talk to and be nice to! Robin, 10

I think the best thing about friendship is that you have someone who will always be there, no matter what. MARGOT, 12

The best thing about friendship is the way we make friends and keep each other's secrets. CAROLYNE. 12

The best thing about friendship is having someone to do stuff with, laugh with and share life's joys with. BROOKE, 12

HOW DO YOU MEASURE AS A FRIEND?

Check off all the traits that describe you as a friend . . .

__ trustworthy

__ nice

__ dependable

__ cheerful

__ funny

__ honest

__ approachable

__ attentive

__ thoughtful

__ kind

__ strong

__ considerate

__ concerned

__ patient

__ generous

__ forgiving

__ loyal

__ caring

__ accommodating

__ likeable

If you scored 0 to 7, you've got to work a little harder to be a better friend to others and yourself.

If you scored 8 to 14, you are well on your way to being a desirable pal.

If you scored 15 to 20, you are tops when it comes to being a buddy!

GIRL TO GIRL

RL

G

RL

GIRL TO GIRL